Mainstreaming the Marginalised

About the Author

V.S. Vyas (PhD Economics) is currently Professor Emeritus in the Institute of Development Studies, Jaipur. He also served as Director, Indian Institute of Management-Ahmedabad (IIM-A). He has taught in prestigious universities and institutions in India and abroad, and worked with the World Bank, Asian Development Bank and FAO, in different capacities. He served as a Member of the Central Board of the Reserve Bank of India and the Economic Advisory Council to the Prime Minister of India. He is the author of several books and articles in the areas of agricultural policy and rural development. He has been honoured by the academic community in India and abroad and was awarded one of the highest national awards, the Padma Bhushan, by the President of India.

Mainstreaming the Marginalised

Reflections on Poverty and Development in Rural India

V.S. VYAS

ACADEMIC FOUNDATION
NEW DELHI

www.academicfoundation.org

First published in 2015
by

ACADEMIC FOUNDATION
4772-73 / 23 Bharat Ram Road, (23 Ansari Road),
Darya Ganj, New Delhi - 110 002 (India).
Phones : 23245001 / 02 / 03 / 04.
Fax : +91-11-23245005.
E-mail : books@academicfoundation.com
www.academicfoundation.org

Cataloging in Publication Data--DK
Courtesy: D.K. Agencies (P) Ltd. <docinfo@dkagencies.com>

Vyas, V. S., author.
Mainstreaming the marginalised : reflections on poverty and development in rural India / V.S. Vyas.
pages cm
ISBN 9789332703148

1. Agriculture and state--India. 2. Rural poor--Government policy--India. 3. Rural development--India. I. Title.

DDC 338.1854 23

Typeset by Italics India, New Delhi.

Printed and bound by The Book Mint, New Delhi.
www.thebookmint.in

Contents

Acknowledgements

Like *Dattatrey* of Hindu mythology, I also have several gurus who have inspired and guided me. For my professional work, I owe a debt of gratitude to my esteemed friend R.J. Bhatia for steering me out of student politics to the study of Economics, and to my teacher and guide Prof M.L. Dantwala for encouraging me to focus on the current and relevant issues of our economy and society.

I am grateful to friends who invited me to express views on issues affecting large sections in our country from an economic perspective, and to Dr Uma Kapila, Chief Editor of the Academic Foundation, for encouraging me to bring out some of my lectures in a book form. I received excellent support from Jyotsana Nambiar, Anju Ddhadda, and particularly from Sona Kapila for editing the pieces with care and patience. My secretary in the Institute of Development Study, Jaipur (IDSJ) Pushpa Kriplani, and Rajesh Sharma in the Ajit Foundation put in hard labour in typing and computing the drafts. I am also thankful to M.I. Khan, Librarian in IDSJ, for the exemplary support he provided at all stages of my work.

In most of the circumstances, one cannot have a long and productive career without the support of members of one's family, especially one's spouse. I am extremely lucky in this respect. To all of them and many unnamed ones my heartfelt thanks.

—V.S. Vyas

Introduction

Over a period of time, I had the good fortune of delivering memorial lectures to honour some distinguished thinkers and activists, and also to speak before my peers in conferences and conventions. On many such occasions, I tried to examine various facets of deprivation and marginalisation, evaluate approaches to correct the inequities, analyse their strength and weaknesses, and suggest conditions that are necessary to achieve the objective of equitable and sustainable growth. Most of my speeches and writings have focused on the rural economy and the rural society. I present, in this volume, some of the lectures and addresses. I am aware of the fact that some changes might have occurred in the situation since what I had depicted in my lectures, but I start with the conviction that my propositions are still largely valid. I should also confess at the outset that there might have been some repetition in my presentations as these are essentially variations on same theme.

I begin this collection with my Verghese Kurien Memorial Lecture titled: "Changing Contours of Rural India: Causes and Consequences" (delivered at the Institute of Rural Management, Anand [IRMA], 2013), where I outlined my understanding of recent changes in the rural society, their causes and consequences. One can point out four powerful forces that are shaping the contemporary rural society. First is the increased accessibility by roads, and now by mobile phones. Isolated, inaccessible villages are becoming a rarity. A rural urban continuum that was a feature of a few regions, most notably of Kerala, is now evident in large parts of the country. Spread of formal education in the countryside has proved the second important change agent. There is a primary school within walking distance; and secondary and high schools have proliferated. Enrolment is practically 100 per cent, although the dropout rate is also very high and quality of education is appalling; but a large section of youth in the villages is exposed to formal education. As I had maintained, these schools have not proved to be 'gateway of knowledge', nonetheless they have changed the attitude and aspirations of the youth. Third major change is the proliferation of government programmes and schemes with the compliment of large staff and ample resources. Besides their intended outcome, this influx of men and material in the rural areas has impacted on the production pattern as well as consumption basket of the rural households. Finally, emergence of *panchayats* as development agents may have created opportunities for decentralised development; it has also created new breeds of politicians and rent-seekers.

These developments have had serious impact on the rural society as well as the economy. In the first place, there has been monetisation of the principal occupation of the rural areas, namely agriculture, on the input as well as the output side. Similarly, consumption pattern has become highly market-oriented. Secondly, there is a marked change in composition of the rural workforce. The proportion of agricultural workers is increasing compared to cultivators, and there is a remarkable change in composition of the non-agricultural workforce, with construction and services flourishing while arts and crafts are decaying. There is also change in the gender composition of the workforce with growing feminisation and a tilt towards an ageing workforce, especially in agriculture. Most importantly, it has resulted in growing income differentiation with the small and marginal farmers with little marketable surplus, thereby being bypassed in an environment of increasing production and favourable terms for agriculture in general.

For more inclusive growth in the rural areas, I have endorsed the strategy of Dr Kurien who wanted small cattle owners to also benefit from what eventually came out as the 'White Revolution'. This strategy comprised: organisation of the poor, exploiting market in favour of the poor, and emphasising human resource development in the rural area.

In the second essay titled: "Challenge of Transforming Indian Agriculture" delivered at the conference of Indian Association of Social Science Institutions (Tarlok Singh Memorial Lecture, Hyderabad, 2011), I discussed the challenge of revitalising Indian agriculture. Despite the satisfactory growth in agricultural production in last few years, two structural deficiencies are becoming apparent. Dependence on agriculture as a source of employment is not decreasing in a remarkable way, although the GDP (gross domestic product) from agriculture has markedly declined. Second, agricultural holding structure is progressively getting dominated by marginal and smallholdings. I also pointed out that growth of productivity in major crops as well as in the subsectors such as dairying and horticulture, is virtually stagnating.

In order to transform our agriculture as a dynamic sector, I envisage that the bulk of growth should come by enabling small farms to be more productive by giving them necessary technical and institutional support. Exit of surplus labour from agriculture should be facilitated by provision of gainful non-farm activities; in other words, by 'pull' factors, rather than 'push' factors. In this context, I discussed the strategy adopted during the Green Revolution, and pointed out its contribution in making the country self-reliant in foodgrains (reasons for its success and some of the resulting problems). In any event, I maintain that we cannot replicate that strategy in the present-day environment as we have become aware of the growing deterioration of the resource base, i.e., land and water, face a different demand pattern for agricultural produce, and find agriculture much more integrated with rest of the economy and the world markets.

For ushering in a small-farm-dominated dynamic agriculture, I suggest three-pronged strategy: enabling marginal and small farmers to enlarge their holdings within the ceiling limits; increasing productivity of small farms; and shifting to high value products with appropriate risk mitigation arrangements. Two pre-conditions are necessary to make this strategy successful. We have to revamp delivery systems in research, extension, marketing and credit, as well as render it small farmer friendly. At the same time, we should encourage and assist cooperative actions with small farmers' organisations, producers' companies or other similar arrangements.

A dynamic agriculture spearheaded by small farm sector will satisfy another requirement for transformation, i.e., diversion of surplus manpower to non-agricultural sectors by generating demand for non-agricultural products. To facilitate such transformation, it is necessary to encourage small and medium industries in the rural areas and encourage larger landholders with resources and enterprise to start non-agricultural enterprises. In this regard, we can learn lessons from China's experience in the early phases of economic reforms in agriculture. To enable such transformation, institutional support for small and tiny rural enterprises will be necessary.

In my Presidential Address to the Annual Conference of the Indian Society of Agriculture Economics, I dwelled on the "Structural Changes in Indian Agriculture" in detail. The discussion was based on the number of holdings and area owned by different size-groups over a period of time. I recognised the limitations of the discussion of agrarian structure on basis of the size-groups of holdings, but maintained that in the rural areas', access to other resources is largely determined by the size of land owned by a household. The other, and practical, reason for selecting size of holdings as reflecting the agrarian structure was that most of the essential information pertaining to agriculture, e.g., cropping pattern, input use, cost of production, etc., is relatively easy to relate with size of holdings.

After examining data from the National Sample Survey (NSS) Rounds pertaining to 1953-54, 1960-61 and 1971-72 (broadly pertaining to 1950s and 1960s), I concluded that: (i) proportion of completely landless household in agricultural workforce was not increasing, (ii) proportion of total marginal holdings to the total holdings as well as proportion of area owned to the total cultivated area by marginal holdings (i.e., those owning less than 1 acre of land) was increasing, (iii) there was no significant change in the proportion of the number of holdings and area owned by the small (owning between 1 to 4.99 acres) and medium (owning between 5 to 14.99 acres) farmers, and (iv) there was a sharp decline in the proportion of big farmers (owning 15 to 49.55 acres) and large farmers (owning more than 50 acres) as well as area owned by them. These trends were observed in practically all states of the country. I drew attention to the fact that since the mid-1950s until beginning of the 1970s, small and medium holdings became numerically more important, while big and large holdings lost their importance in terms of number as well as area owned.

These changes in the structure of holdings occurred due to demographic pressures, land reforms and market processes. In the absence of non-farm employment, increase in population led to sub-division and fragmentation of holdings. Incidence of sub-division was felt more on big and large holdings. Land reforms, though badly implemented, did lead to disposal of land by big and large farmers, especially the absentee owners, who owned land more than that permitted by the land ceiling legislation. The land market was mostly inert but wherever it was active, big and large farmers were more likely to be the sellers, and small and medium farmers to be the buyers.

While concluding the lecture I also referred to an ongoing study, in which I was involved, that looked into the effects of inequality of landholdings, as measured by the Gini coefficient, in different agro-ecological regions, on per hectare value of the farm output. Our tentative conclusion was that inequity in landholdings was creating a negative effect on the per hectare value of the output, except in a crop like wheat where a highly productive technology could overcome handicaps imposed by an unequal landholding structure.

Summing up the discussion, I concluded: "even in our present system enough pressures could be generated by legislative and administrative processes enabling small farmers in the countryside to hold on their own." At the same time I also recognised that: "While structural changes of the type described earlier were meant to help agricultural growth, the net outcome judged in terms of production was not at all satisfactory."

In an earlier discussion on the same theme, in my Presidential Address to Gujarat Economic Association (1975), titled: "Structural Change in Agriculture and the Small Farm Sector in Gujarat", I looked in depth at the changes taking place in the agrarian structure of Gujarat, and their causes and consequences. Examination of the state-level data, as reported in relevant NSS Rounds (16 and 26), Population Census and Agricultural Census (latter pertaining to 1971), and three carefully conducted micro-level studies led to the conclusion that increase in the number and proportion of agricultural workers in the rural workforce did not reflect a process of prolitarianisation, i.e., sequestering land of the small and marginal landowners by large capitalist farmers resulting in a growing army of the landless workers, even though there was evidence of growing immiseration.

I suggested that growth in number of agricultural workers was due to increase in that of the household members, all of those who could not be supported by the marginal and small holdings. They had to seek work outside their holding; and in the absence of non-farm employment opportunities, the only alternative was to work as agricultural workers. Important point was that the small farmers were not losing land, they were clinging to their petty holdings.

I maintained that the land reforms in Gujarat were indirectly responsible for this situation. The land ceiling legislation in Gujarat did not yield any sizable area of land for redistribution, but it made further expansion of holding very risky. In several parts of the state, Tenancy Legislation with the objective of "Land to the Tiller" did benefit small tenants, especially those cultivating land of the absentee landowners. Due to the fear of ceiling and tenancy legislation, land market—to the extent it was active—did favour the small and marginal farmers.

Lest it is considered as an over-optimistic view, I also showed that the small and marginal farmers could retain their land and several of them could marginally increase their holdings, but it did not contribute to their prosperity. They were operating on a thin production base, did not have resources to invest for improving it, were discriminated against availing credit and modern inputs, and were handicapped in marketing their small surplus. Perusal of the relevant studies showed that they were largely growing low value crops, and yields of the small share of 'commercial crops' on these holdings were lower than average yields of the region. Contrary to the prevailing view, I maintained that inverse size productivity relationship did not operate as far as the small farm sector of Gujarat was concerned.

I concluded my address suggesting that it was possible to treat the small farm sector as a surplus-generating sector, as was the case in most of the Southeast Asian countries. But for that to happen, we need to consider alternative institutional arrangements so as to provide credit and modern inputs to small farms and generate appropriate technologies for them.

In my Presidential Address to the Indian Society of Labour Economics, titled: "Marginalised Sections of Indian Agriculture: The Forgotten Millions" (delivered at Bharathidasan University, 2007), once again I reverted to the theme of marginal farmers and their economy. I looked into the extent of marginal holdings and their growth overtime and in different states, depicted status of their economy with the help of some indicators, reviewed programmes meant to make an impact on their economy, and discussed possible measures to improve their income.

I started with underlining two important phenomena: slow pace of urbanisation and overwhelming dependence on agriculture for livelihood in the rural areas. Within agriculture, as I had noted in my earlier writings, number as well as area under marginal holdings were increasing. This tendency was reflected in each of the NSS Rounds from the early 1970s to the mid-1990s. By 1995-96, over 71 million holdings were accounted by marginal holdings (of 1 ha or less), and they cultivated about 17 per cent of the land. I postulated then that by 2005-06, nearly 14 million holdings would be added to this category, and area cultivated could amount to more than 20 per cent of the total cultivated area. During the period under review, the number of marginal holdings had increased in practically every state. Their major concentration was in Uttar Pradesh (UP), Bihar and Andhra Pradesh (AP). Only significant exception was Punjab.

Factors bringing about changes in landholding structure were the same as mentioned in my previous lectures, namely, land reforms, land markets and demographic pressure. An additional factor discouraging expansion of holdings by medium and large farmers was the input intensive, high-value agriculture opted by these categories of farmers rather than investment in additional land. I reiterated that the operation of the 'ladder' phenomenon, i.e., landless acquiring small piece of land and marginal farmers graduating to small farmer category by the same process, did operate in small parts of the country. But that had not affected the preponderance of marginal farmers.

Next I turned to the economy of marginal cultivators. As far as income from land is concerned—prices remaining same—it largely depends on the quality of land, cropping pattern, and quality and quantity of the inputs used. I maintained that on all these counts, marginal farmers faced disadvantages. For this group, agricultural labour was another important source of income. But it was not an expanding source, as by all evidence elasticity of employment with respect to output growth in agriculture was near zero.

Dairying and animal husbandry emerged as the most important ancillary activity. The marginal farmers had relative advantage in dairying with availability of open grazing land, adequate labour supply and an expanding market. This advantage was now disappearing with shrinkage of open land and replacement of a higher value dairy animal (buffalo) in place of low value animal (cow) with the former also requiring larger resources for maintenance.

In the given situation, I suggested a three-pronged strategy. I reiterated that to improve the lot of this large and disadvantaged section in agriculture—what I had termed as the 'forgotten millions'—we have to increase and improve asset base of the small and marginal farmers; improve productivity on these farms; and increase scope for non-farm employment. This strategy would succeed to the extent supportive institutions in research, extension credit and marketing assist this large section of agricultural producers. The marginal farmers need to organise to avail various facilities and measures to mitigate risks in production and marketing. I concluded that time was ripe to usher in a vibrant small farm sector by adopting a more focused approach towards this segment of our agriculture.

In my V.V. Giri Memorial Lecture delivered at the Conference of Indian Society of Labour Economics (Institute of Development Studies, Jaipur, 2004), I dwelled on the issue of agrarian distress, which was very much in news because of a spate of farmers' suicide. I maintained that the poor are more prone to market-induced as well as natural disasters over and above the household level calamities, because their capacity to face the disasters is very low. I found that even in 1999-2000 more than 26 per cent of the rural population was counted as poor, while the unofficial estimates put even a higher figure. There was greater concentration of the poor and hence vulnerable in three large states, UP, Bihar and Madhya Pradesh (MP) and a large majority of these belonged to SCs (scheduled castes) and STs (scheduled tribes).

Agricultural labourers and marginal farmers accounted for 48 per cent and 28 per cent of the poor in the rural areas respectively .

Indian agriculture was undergoing a slow but steady transformation. Cropping pattern had changed in favour of commercial crops, while share of purchased inputs was progressively increasing. In regions where high value crops such as Bt cotton, were grown, farmers' dependence on product as well as on input markets was escalating. This made agricultural producers more vulnerable to market fluctuations. A trend in liberalisation of external trade exposed Indian farmers to external shocks as well.

This period was also characterised by low productivity, especially as compared to the productivity surge in 1970s and 1980s. Deceleration in productivity had to be viewed in face of higher doses and higher prices of the inputs. Researchers had shown that once the input like fertiliser or pesticide crossed the 'low utilisation level', diminishing returns started. It was a period when output prices showed much larger fluctuation around a mildly declining trend. In that situation, some regions and sections of the rural population suffered more. Those affected included farmers and agricultural labourers in rainfed areas, marginal farmers all over the country and commercial farmers who went for heavy doses of purchased inputs. I maintained that these vulnerable sections and regions needed greater attention. Most of these groups had to contract large loans from informal sector, mainly moneylenders, who charged high rate of interest and used coercive methods to recover loans. Under these circumstances, many self-respecting farmers had taken the extreme step of committing suicide to save face.

To ameliorate the plight of these sections, I discussed a strategy comprising: instituting credible risk mitigating measures; investing in improvement of the quality and quantity of land and water resources; and strengthening supportive institutions, especially for extension and credit. As an immediate measure, I suggested that the formal financial institutions should take over debts of the farmers from usurious sources and lighten their interest burden.

The lecture delivered under the auspices of BASIX Academy for Livelihood and Micro Banking Practice in Hyderabad (2014) titled:

"Towards an Equitable Agrarian Structure", sums up my views on a desirable agrarian structure and strategies to achieve this goal.

Availability of later data validated my earlier conclusions on the increasing area under small and marginal holdings and processes, which were leading to this outcome. I also reiterated that agriculture on most of these holdings was not viable and that only with agriculture labour and dairying, the small and marginal farmers were able to survive. The prospects for the latter were also not bright. On the other hand, semi-medium and medium farms were not only surviving, but were probably leading agricultural growth in the country. Policy thrust should therefore be to expand the share of these medium holdings.

To achieve this objective, I suggested simultaneous action on several fronts. These would comprise expanding opportunities for non-farm employment for very small, 'handkerchief' holding for whom there was no future in agriculture and encouraging them to lease or sell off their land; providing opportunities to the potentially viable small and marginal farmers to expand their holdings by leasing-in or purchase of land; and encouraging and helping large farmers to lease-out or sale their land and in starting rural non-farm enterprises. I maintained that involvement of large farmers and very small farmers in agricultural production was already declining, even though their sources of non-farm income were different. Agriculture and non-agricultural labour in one case, and rent, moneylending and trade on the other. But in the absence of clear vision and direction, the process was yielding sub-optimal results.

To achieve desirable results, we could not rely on confiscatory land reforms, which in any case had a chequered history. New phase of reforms would have to be market-friendly, with active support of the state to ensure that market bias against the poor was discouraged. In this scenario, state should be playing active part in the land market in favour of the poor, the way it was intervening in support of large industries.

Finally, I submitted that proposed changes in agrarian structure could not be carried out without active support from credit, marketing and extension agencies. We should not leave the new beneficiaries of reforms to their own devices; the mistake we had committed in the earlier phase of the land reforms.

In the next two sections of the book, I present my views on food security. First of these is R.S. Bhatt Memorial Lecture titled: "Food Security in India: Can We Eliminate Hunger and Malnutrition in Foreseeable Future" (delivered under the auspices of the Bhavnagar University, 2005). I started with the premise that in a civilised society, everyone deserves to be food secure. I also pointed out that there was general agreement on the definition of food security, which could be interpreted as "access to adequate food to all people at all times for an active and healthy life." In the light of the above, then prevailing scenario suggested that:

- Hunger, in terms of starvation, had been largely eliminated, although there was a disturbingly large extent of seasonal hunger, especially in rainfed areas.
- A large proportion of the rural household subsisted on less than 1,800 calories per person per day, which could be considered minimum calorie requirement for an active life.
- There had been no progress in ensuring nutritional security for young children, lactating mothers and elderly persons without any family support.

In order to achieve universal food and nutritional security in the country, I reviewed the policies and programmes addressed to achieve the same. As far as policies were concerned, we emphasised on the availability of foodgrains from domestic production. I maintained that as long as a large section of producers depended on the production of foodgrains and food occupied a large share in consumers' expenditure, the policy of food self-sufficiency was justified.

We also had a network of public distribution shops to make it possible to access food at all times at all places. There were also viable policy measures to ensure that sharp fluctuations in prices are avoided. The procurement of foodgrains at MSPs (minimum support prices) and their distribution through PDS (public distribution system) coupled with buffer stock operations could ensure reasonably stable prices. With the launching of EGS (employment guarantee scheme), the poor got the entitlement to have required quantity of foodgrains. Thus, a policy package was available to provide food security. The only gap in the policy was due to its cereal-centric approach, which failed to address the issues of nutritional security. I also raised questions about the sustainability of our policy of 'cheap inputs-cheap output' involving subsidies to the producers as well the consumers of foodgrains.

The major lacunae, however, were in the design and implementation of the programmes. I referred in that connection the three major programmes addressed to achieve the objective of food security, namely, PDS and its variants, Integrated Child Development Scheme (ICDS) and Mid-Day Meals (MDM) scheme. Recognising their contribution in ensuring food security, I pointed out their defects.

Next I turned to the major gap in our approach to food and nutritional security, neglect of health and sanitation concerns. I reiterated that, "With totally inadequate health care and deteriorating environmental conditions, intake of nutritious food is no better than storing water in a sieve."

In the end, I suggested measures to make the programmes viable for ensuring continuous availability of food, stability in food prices and accessibility of food for all sections of the society. I also suggested a series of measures to improve nutritional security. I concluded that, "neither dearth of resources nor lack of experience can be cited as reasons for further delaying the task of ensuring a Food Secure India."

The I.P. Desai Memorial Lecture delivered at the Centre for Social Studies, Surat (2013), was titled: "Reaching the Unreached: To Make Poverty Alleviation Programmes More Effective". At the outset, I posed the question that despite good intentions backed by considerable resources and a variety of programmes, why we were unable to substantially reduce the number of poor households in our country. I pointed out limitations of the poverty estimates including those based on income, rather than consumption, criterion; but made it clear that whatever criteria are accepted, there is a large number of poor and deprived households.

Discussion on poverty alleviation in our country should take into account the fact that we had registered a reasonably fast growth, but benefits of growth were not percolating to the lowest strata of society. I hypothesised that poor were not in a position to take advantage of the growth-induced opportunities principally as they did not possess income-generating assets, latter including physical assets, stamina to labour, skill to meet market demand and access to financial or social capital. Programmes for poverty alleviation should correct these deficiencies.

The other set of programmes were those aimed at creating capabilities among the poor so that they may come out of the 'poverty trap'. Among these, the more important ones were: food and nutrition security, access to education and skill formation, ensuring health, subsidised housing and support to special categories of the poor, e.g., ST and SC, minorities, etc. All these programmes met with less than expected success, especially if one was looking at benefits to the marginalised sections. In order to reach these sections, I dwelled on four missing links: appropriate design of the programmes, reforming delivery systems, building collective strength of the poor and creating an enabling environment. I concluded that to leave one-third of the population behind in our quest for higher growth couldn't be justified by any cannon of ethics. It was also bad economics, as sustainable growth even in terms of GDP will remain elusive with such high burden of marginalised households.

In next two sections, I turn to issues which go beyond economic calculations. These may contribute to what I had called earlier as 'enabling environment'. First of these relate to democratic values and the role of civil society. In my Mohan Singh Mehta Memorial Lecture (delivered at Seva Mandir, Udaipur, 2003), titled: "Weakening Roots of Democracy and the Role of Civil Society", I dwelled on the reasons why, at the time of independence, India opted for democratic form of government and how over a period of time distortions had set in at different levels. I then proceeded to spell out the conditions that are necessary to have genuine democracy, and the role that civil society institutions can play in meeting those conditions.

I held that the traditions of plurality and tolerance in Indian culture, broad participation of the masses in freedom struggle, and the liberal and western-oriented leadership during the independence movement were the key factors in establishing a democratic form of government in our country after independence. However, our adherence to democracy is limited to outward symbols, such as universal suffrage, multiparty political system and elections with regular periodicity. Two essential features of genuine democracy, rule of law and civil liberties, are seriously compromised.

Progressive deterioration in the democratic values is partly due to complexity of some of the modern institutions. The best examples of these will be the central monetary authority and defence establishments, which preclude possibility of 'governance by the people'. There are other defects, which have crept up over the period of time. These include executive's tendency to evade the legislative wing, falling standards of the legislators, growing distance between the peoples' representatives and the common man, and above all rampant corruption which is taken for granted by the society.

Next, I tried to underline the conditions that are necessary for strengthening the roots of democracy. These include: transparency and accountability in functioning of every institution; ensuring democratic functioning of major institutions outside government such as judiciary, press, political parties, as well a strong and fair government; participatory and functioning government at all levels (from village to the centre); equality of opportunity for every citizen; inculcating value of tolerance and giving it place of pride in every aspect of social and political life. I also maintained that in this interdependent world, it is equally important to democratise world-level institutions. I emphasised that the root of democracy is nourished by a set of values and not merely by institutional arrangements.

I tried to underline the role of civil society institutions, especially NGOs (non-governmental organisations), in this context. Their role could be identified in three areas: advocacy, protest and innovative initiatives. It is expected that they would bring the advantages of various schemes and programmes to the sections and areas which are generally bypassed. Their advocacy should go beyond schemes and programmes; they should also be active in advocating democratic values and human rights. They should protest whenever there are acts of injustice, particularly against the deprived sections. They can also play the role of innovators in finding new ways to assist the poor. But for successfully performing all these roles, they have to practise transparency and hold themselves accountable to the public at large. I concluded that commitment to democracy is essential in itself; efforts to resolve the problems, which are weakening the roots of democracy, are equally important.

Last contribution in this volume is an enlarged and revised version of my Bhailal Bhai Patel Memorial Lecture (delivered under the auspices of Sardar Patel University, Vallabh Vidyanagar, 1979), titled: "Academics as Activists: An Indian Perspective on Action Research in Rural Development". This lecture was based on my experience in action research as a member of Indian Institute of Management (IIM)-Ahmedabad faculty team, which started an action research project (Dharampur Project) in one of the most backward talukas of Gujarat. The project was named Rural Development for Rural Poor.

I maintained that in a country such as India, demands on academics go far beyond their role in classroom or laboratory. Many have opted to respond to these demands, without resigning from their primary role as teachers or researchers, getting involved and observing the development process in organisations or communities. This type of research commonly known as action research implies giving equal emphasis on experience and reflection, on conceptualisation and implementation. In the context of rural development, it has also a bias towards deprived sections. An academic as an activist involved in rural development focusing on the poor should have long-term commitments; some skills to assist the community; should not aspire for a leadership role; and should be prepared to take responsibility for his or her action. Above all, the participant should not forget his or her principal function as a teacher and a researcher.

One can trace the history of action research, of the type I had discussed as Gandhian educational movement, in pre-Independence India. The *ashram shalas* sponsored by the followers of Mahatma Gandhi imparted 'basic'—craft-centred, ethical—education to the rural people. The individuals who were part of this educational system performed the role of 'trinity': learners, instructors and implementers.

There is a recent revival of interest among academics in action research. Their involvement ranges from joining the radical movements to mass awakening and conscientisation, to action research of academic type as described above. In this lecture, I was focusing more on the last category.

Academic activists have different arrangements with their parent institutions in terms of time to be spent in field and responsibilities to be undertaken in their core teaching and research activities. In their role as activist, academics start with several advantages and, also face several handicaps. Despite the atmosphere of cynicism, academics in our society enjoy greater respect, more so among the marginalised sections. Their access to bureaucracy, especially in non-metropolitan areas, is much easier. Similarly, they have relative advantage in getting cooperation from other development agencies. They can take more pragmatic view and can offer fresh ideas and approaches without being 'prisoners of precedents'. The point most in favour of the academics in this regard is that their experience makes it easy for them to establish rapport with young people.

Academics have serious handicaps while accepting the role of activists. These should not be ignored. To start with, their social background is more likely to be different from the marginalised groups with whom they intend to work. This places a constraint in their functioning. The major limitation is placed due to the conflict between the career goals and ideological predilection. Involvement in action research does not directly subserve the career goals. Besides, by nature of their training and by tradition, academics—particularly in social sciences—are 'lone wolf', while rural development is a team effort. In dealing with multitude of organisations and with politicians of different colour and hue, academics are at disadvantages. Their training and background do not equip them to cope with situations of open conflicts, power sharing, bargaining and trade-offs.

I concluded that the advantages of action research by academics far outweigh handicaps and are beneficial to the disadvantaged sections as well to the researcher, provided two conditions are satisfied—the researcher should have genuine concern for the poor, and the experience gained in the field should be reflected in teaching and research.

To conclude, following are the main messages these presentations convey: a large number of rural households are marginalised and their number is increasing; there is a possibility of reversing the trend by appropriate policy initiatives, and more importantly by strengthening the delivery systems; an enabling environment can be created so that the marginalised sections not only get benefits from growth, but also contribute to growth.

1

Changing Contours of Rural India

*Causes and Consequences**

This paper focuses on the changing contours of rural India, where we have gone right and where we have failed. I have, in the paper, referred mainly to the period after 2000, i.e., the changes one can observe in the new millennium. I must mention at the beginning that I am painting a macro picture that too in broad strokes. In a vast country like ours, every statement can be countered by referring to some specific region or a particular section. I am aware of this. Yet, I see some merit in taking an overall view of our rural scene so that others who want to go for details can appreciate the background and the context.

I

I start by identifying some of the developments, which have made a profound impact on rural economy in our country; spell out the outcome of these changes, i.e., the strengths they have imparted and distortions they have led to; and finally suggest a few critical areas where we should focus if we have to come close to Dr Kurien's dream of improving the lives of rural people in general and small men and women in particular.

Among several important forces of change, I have focused on four major developments that are shaping contemporary rural economy and society. These are: (i) increased connectivity, (ii) spread of formal education, (iii) plethora of government programmes with large funds and numerous functionaries, and (iv) emergence of *panchayats* as powerful political institutions. Let me say a few words on each of these.

---

*: Edited version of Dr Varghese Kurien Memorial Lecture delivered at Institute of Rural Management (IRMA), Anand, 13 December 2013.

Increased Connectivity: The most important among recent developments is the growing accessibility in rural areas. The existence of an isolated, inaccessible village is now becoming a rarity. The attempt to link all villages with all-weather roads started in right earnest in the year 2000 with the Pradhan Mantri Gram Sadak Yojana (PMGSY), which aimed at providing paved road initially to villages with a population of above 1,000, and eventually to all villages with over 500 inhabitants. This programme got a fillip once it became a component of the ambitious Bharat Nirman Programme. In more recent years, Mahatma Gandhi National Rural Employment Guarantee Act (MGNREGA), the nation's flagship programme for rural India, has also contributed significantly to the road-building programme. The net result is that more than three-fourth of India's villages are connected by roads on which a motorised vehicle can play. Most of these roads are fair-weather roads and the vehicles playing on them are ramshackle buses and lorries, but connectivity is assured for an overwhelmingly large majority of villages. This has resulted in the phenomenon of rural-urban continuum, a situation that is now observable in many parts of the country, not only in Kerala.

The impact of greater connectivity on the rural economy is far reaching. In a series of studies, which the Ministry of Rural Development had instituted in eight states in 2006 to assess the impact of road connectivity on agriculture, it was revealed that it had made substantial and positive difference on every aspect of agricultural production and marketing. Better connectivity has also led to increase in non-farm employment opportunities, small industries, trade and services. Of course, this has also enabled urban enterprises to introduce their products and services in the rural areas with much ease, most of the time at the cost of local artisans and traditional service providers.

More than surface connectivity, it is the spread of telecommunication which is changing the face of rural India. The country has recorded one of the fastest growths of telephony in the world, and rural areas have their adequate share. According to the Telecom Regulatory Authority of India (TRAI), by July 2012, there were more than 904 million telephone subscribers in India. Of these, nearly 40 per cent, roughly 360 million, were in rural areas, and the number of rural subscribers is rapidly increasing. A farmer ploughing a field or transporting his product to a nearby market with his cell phone glued to his ear is not an unusual sight. With the extension of broadband facilities under the ambitious National Optical Fiber Network and spread of IT applications, rural India is undergoing a veritable communication revolution.[1]

Spread of Formal Education: Another major development taking place in rural India is the spread of formal education. During the last few decades, the education landscape of rural India has changed beyond recognition. Now there is a school practically in every village, and near universal enrolment of children of school-going age. (However retention of boys and girls in schools after the first few years, and quality of education are still major problems, as I will observe later.) Even now the difference between the literacy rates in urban (83.6% male and 73.6% females in 2009-10) and rural India (70.6% males and 53.3% females, in the same year) is significant, but it is fast narrowing; Sarva Shikshya Abhiyan (SSA) has covered the whole of India, including the rural areas, making it easier for boys and girls to get elementary education. Schemes such as Mid-Day Meal (MDM) have further helped the enrolment of boys and girls in schools. The Right to Education (RTE) Act, which came into force in April 2010, aiming at eight years of compulsory education for all children, will further accelerate the spread of education in rural areas.

Educational institutions of all levels are spreading rapidly in the rural areas. There is a primary school within walking distance in large parts of the country. The number of secondary schools is burgeoning. Practically every taluka/tehsil town has a college. Apart from the government's efforts, the private sector is making its presence felt in the education field. Even in rural areas, privately run 'English medium' schools are becoming ubiquitous. An all-India survey conducted in 2005 found that 21 per cent of rural children were enrolled in private schools (Desai *et al.*, 2010). Since then the proportion must have

1 A study of the National Centre for Agricultural Policy Research in Agriculturally Backward and Developed Areas in Haryana (reported in their *Annual Report for 2012-13*) found that three-fourth of farmers were using their mobile phones for information on availability and prices of inputs and marketing their output.

risen significantly. Presence of private sector is more prominent in the secondary level institutions. The Twelfth Plan notes that nearly half the secondary schools in the country are sponsored by the private sector. With an increase in the number of secondary schools and colleges in the rural areas, the number of people passing out from these institutions has also increased. By 2009-10, 18.8 per cent of rural males and 10.3 per cent of rural females had education up to secondary level and above (NSS, 66th Round, 2009-10).

Admittedly, infrastructure of the educational institutions in rural areas is grossly inadequate; they are under-staffed and the quality of teaching is appalling. Schooling in most of these institutions does open the 'gateway to knowledge,' yet the students who go through these institutions, especially those who get secondary and college education, imbibe a different worldview from their parents. They may not acquire higher knowledge, but their aspiration level changes. Due to lack of relevance and poor quality, the spread of education in rural India might not have made any measurable impact on the production processes or employment opportunities, but it has resulted in truly distinguishable consumption patterns and living style bringing rural population, particularly the youth, closer to their urban counterparts.

Large Influx of Public Servants: The pace of change in rural areas has accelerated with the massive intrusion of public institutions and their functionaries. Historically, state administration ended at the district level with a few functionaries, mainly the revenue and police officers, stationed at the lower level. The picture has completely changed now. With the government assuming a major role in economic and social development, a plethora of programmes and schemes are located in the administrative units below the district, right up to the village level. The Departments of Health, Education, Social Security, Women Empowerment and many more have their functionaries in villages. Other development departments like Irrigation, Power and Roads, to name a few, are also present in villages.

Apart from the government departments, a number of public agencies are increasingly being located in rural areas. Post offices already had a very wide coverage of the rural areas. Fair price shops numbering thousands have been located in the rural areas. Now more than one-fourth of the villages have branches or correspondents of commercial banks. There are more than 1,00,000 cooperative credit societies located in rural areas. Overall nearly 2,68,000 banking outlets have been set up in the villages as on March 2013 (Chakrabarty, 2013). A large number of NBFCs (non-banking financial companies), chit funds and insurance companies have located their offices or appointed agents in the rural areas. In every part of the country, hundreds of public functionaries are working in the units below a district, in taluka/tehsils' headquarters and even in villages. Way back, in 1980, as part of Indian Institute of Management's (IIM's) project on Rural Development for Rural Poor, we conducted a survey in a backward tehsil of Rajasthan, Devagarh. We found that there were 27 agencies working in that tehsil accounting for 570 functionaries. Similar results were obtained in our survey of a backward taluka of Gujarat, Dharampur. Since then the number of agencies and their staff located in rural areas must have increased many fold.

I am not commenting on the development role or efficiency or probity of these functionaries. What I wish to point out is that this army of officials is acting as change agents in rural areas with its distinct lifestyle and higher spending power. Most of these functionaries are urban educated youth who import urban values and lifestyle to rural areas. Their higher spending power affects the production and employment structure in the rural areas. As their number is progressively increasing, their impact on rural society is also becoming more pronounced.

Emergence of Panchayats as Power Centres: A profound change has occurred in rural life with enactment of the 73rd amendment to the Constitution, which provides constitutional status to the three-tier Panchayati Raj Institutions (PRIs), at the district, block and village levels. Several features of this institution have introduced significant changes in rural life, especially at the village level. For example, there is a provision for regular meetings of the village general assembly, *gram sabha*, regular elections of the *panchayats*, 50 per cent reservation for women in the *panchayats* and so on. All these are meant to give power to villagers including women. It is true that only a minority of the *panchayats* lives up to its constitutional responsibility, but in every state, some sections of more alert or resourceful persons are assuming power through this route.

There is a constitutional provision to delegate 29 important functions of the state, such as education, health, social services, etc., to these institutions. Not all the states in the country have delegated these functions to *panchayats,* but a beginning has been made in several states. With the delegation of these responsibilities, there is a demand for giving funds and functionaries to carry out various activities. The *panchayats* now have large funds at their disposal and a sizable number of employees under their supervision.

More important than the delegated functions, the 'agency' function has made them very powerful institutions. A number of government schemes, the most important among these being MGNREGA, are executed by the *panchayats*. For a few other central schemes, funds are directly given to the *panchayats*, bypassing the states. It is not uncommon to find a village *panchayat* handling an annual budget of ₹80-100 million. Such large sums of money spent in the villages under the supervision of the elected representatives have changed the village environments as well as the status of the elected *panchs*. Although huge amounts under control of the *panchayats* has not necessarily led to more efficient or honest use of money, it has, however, given rise to a new breed of leaders in the village with substantial power.

II

Let us now look into how these changes have affected the village society. Cumulative effect of these developments is reflected, principally, in monetisation of the rural economy, changes in the structure and composition of rural workforce, and increasing prosperity along with growing income differentiation in rural areas.

Penetration of Market: Because of easy transport and communication facilities, commercialisation has made deep inroads in the rural area. In the main economic activity in rural areas, i.e., agriculture, which accounts for 66.5 per cent of the rural workforce, the share of purchased inputs is progressively increasing. An earlier symbol of Indian agriculture, a farmer walking behind a wooden plough drawn by a pair of bullocks with a family member assisting in the farming operations, has to be replaced by a farmer driving a tractor, using large amounts of purchased inputs and hiring labour for major farm operations. Farming, which was principally dependent on family labour and family-owned inputs, has now become an activity largely relying on purchased inputs and services. The amount of expenditure on fertilisers, pesticides, purchased seeds, diesel and electricity has been increasing year by year.

At the output level, the shift to commercialisation is even more pronounced. High value, market-oriented products of allied sectors to agriculture, namely horticulture, dairy and animal husbandry, poultry and fishery already account for 50 per cent of the total value of the output of agriculture, and their share is progressively increasing. In the crop sector too, the so-called 'commercial crops', e.g., cotton, oilseeds, sugarcane, etc., are acquiring a dominant share, relegating foodgrain production to a secondary place. Due to the increased share of the purchased inputs and larger proportion of output for sale in the market, agriculture's backward as well as forward links with the rest of the economy are becoming ever stronger (Mythili and Hara, 2013). Compared to the inputs and products, the consumption pattern has become even more market oriented. In the consumption basket of rural families, the share of non-food, non-agricultural commodities and services are dominating.

The picture of self-reliant (for production) and self-sufficient (in consumption) rural households has become outdated. Market forces have an impact on their livelihood as well as on household economy with ever-increasing intensity. The lesson is clear: while formulating macro policies for credit, trade, pricing, etc., their impact on rural livelihood and rural consumption cannot be ignored.

Changing Composition of Workforce: Easy accessibility has facilitated market penetration in the rural areas; it has also affected composition of the workforce. An immediate result has been the growing feminisation of agriculture. Men folk leaving villages in hordes every morning for a nearby town in overcrowded buses for wage labour and returning in the evening with paltry earnings is a common sight in large parts of the country. Meanwhile, the women have to look after the households as well as their small farms. Actual work on the farms by women is underestimated if one takes into account only the 'principle source of income' criterion. In 2012-13, on MGNREGA sites in the country as a whole, women accounted for 51 per cent of labour days; and in seven states, including Kerala, Goa, Tamil Nadu (TN), Rajasthan and Andhra Pradesh (AP), the proportion of women workers was more than the national average. Thus, wage-paid labour on MGNREGA may be their principal source of income, but women manage most of the small family farms, mostly as unpaid family workers.

Another factor changing the composition of workforce, in this case a tilt towards more elderly people, is results of the spread of education in rural areas. It is not only because the youth, especially boys, are in school that they are not available for work. Even after rudimentary schooling, they are reluctant to work on the farm. The fact of progressive feminisation of farming is now well recognised. A less appreciated, though an equally important, phenomenon is the growing proportion of the aged among the workers. The National Sample Survey (NSS) 60th Round has shown that the proportion of rural male workers in the age group of 60 and above has increased from 70 per 1,000 workers in 1999-2000 to 77 in 2009-10. The rise in the proportion of female rural workers in the same age group during that period was 72 per 1,000 to 81 per 1,000. The reverse phenomenon, i.e., declining proportion in the workforce, is observed in the 20-29 age group. If the present trend continues, the proportion of aged in the rural workforce may become higher still as 'education' spreads in the rural areas, making youth reluctant to work on farms.

Diversification of Occupational Structure: With all these developments, one sensitive indicator of change, namely diversification of occupation structure, does not seem to have changed much. For the country as whole, the dependence on agriculture as the main source of livelihood has declined from 58 per cent to 51 per cent over a decade, from 2001 to 2011. For a fast-developing economy, averaging GDP (gross domestic product) growth of 8-9 per cent per year, this does not appear as a remarkable change. However, it does not reflect fully the changes occuring in rural occupational structure. For example, there has been significant change in composition of the agricultural workforce. Proportion of 'workers' in the agricultural workforce is progressively increasing and that of 'farmers' is declining.

This increase in the proportion of workers should be viewed, as I will explain later, in the context of diminution of the size of holdings. Available evidence suggests that larger proportion of SCs (scheduled castes), STs (scheduled tribes) and minority community households are changing their principal source of livelihood, i.e., cultivation to farm and non-farm labour (NSSO, 66th Round).

Equally significant changes have taken place in the composition of workforce in the rural non-agricultural sectors. Number of workers engaged in small household enterprises, i.e., in traditional arts and crafts, is declining. Rural workers engaged in trade, transport and construction have increased. Prosperity of a section of rural society and the changing lifestyle of the rural households has affected the occupational composition in the non-farm sector in the rural area. Taking advantage of these developments, the organised sector, including large MNCs, from soft-drink makers to white goods manufacturers, has also penetrated rural areas to push their wares.

Increasing Prosperity and Growing Differentiation: On the whole, rural areas have benefited from these changes. Rural incomes have increased, poverty has been reduced, productivity in agriculture (in value terms) has improved, and terms of trade have gone in favour of agriculture. Whether in terms of income per hectare or income per worker, there is an improvement over a period of time. Apart from the favourable stance of policy directly impinging on agriculture, such as MSPs (minimum support prices), subsidised inputs and credit, the overall economic reforms, e.g., privatisation and trade liberalisation have also benefited agriculture sector (Vyas, 2000).

The overall picture of rural prosperity, however, hides substantial misery and deprivation of a section of the rural people. There is wide differentiation in wealth and income in the rural society. Based on the NSS consumption data, a recent study has concluded that inter-personal inequality has increased in the country as well as in the rural areas. In the rural areas, sharp and persistent inequality can be observed between farm and non-farm sectors, rainfed and irrigated agriculture, marginal farmers and middle & large farmers, marginal and small farmers, and middle and large farmers (Motiram and Vakulabharanam, 2013). The marginal and small farmers are particularly handicapped. As I have elaborated elsewhere,[2] despite of being at a serious disadvantage in the market place, the government schemes leave them to their fate too. The official figures on rural poverty do not take into account the households who are only marginally above the poverty line and are vulnerable to shocks: market-induced, natural, familial or personal. In terms of numbers, disadvantaged sections in the rural areas far outweigh those who have benefited from the developments I mentioned earlier.

A powerful factor contributing to the income as well as social differentiation is a politicisation of rural society. The starting point is the election to *panchayats*, which carries not only prestige but also control over vast resources. It also facilitates contacts with state bureaucracy and managers of the public institutions, and ensures benefits that may be obtained from such contacts. Political parties also like to gain a foothold in rural areas by controlling the *panchayats* directly, or by proxies. Ensuring competition for power aggravates the differentiation in rural society.

The problem of 'rural-urban divide' is voiced at several fora. However, an equally serious problem of 'rural-rural divide' does not receive as much attention. As a matter of fact, benefits of state policies and programmes are pre-empted by a section of the rural society, while the rest have to remain content with paltry relief.

III

The changes discussed earlier have affected different sections of rural society in different ways. While a number of geographically and socially well-placed households gain all the positive advantages from these changes, many others have been left behind and even become losers. To ensure that the gains are shared more equitably, the strategy adopted by Dr Kurien in developing AMUL has great relevance in the present context. As I understand it, there are three pillars of this strategy: organisation of the producers, taking advantage of the

2 *Marginalised Sections of Indian Agriculture: The Forgotten Millions*, Presidential Address to 48th Conference of Indian Society of Labour Economics 2007.

existing and the potential demand, and emphasis on human resource development.

Organisation of the Poor: The reasons the marginalised groups of rural society are not able to take advantage of the recent developments are: (i) the high transaction cost involved and (ii) weak bargaining power. With collective action, the poor can largely overcome these disadvantages.

One of the common problems of the poor, the urban as well as the rural, is that as individuals they have no identities, and no bargaining power. In the market place, they are always losers, whether it is in the labour market or in the market for goods and services. Besides, there are activities, which may be profitably organised only if scale is imparted to them. These handicaps can be overcome with some form of collective organisation.

We have experience with different forms of organisations for collective action, e.g., SHGs (self-help groups), cooperatives, producer companies, etc. Not many of these organisations have succeeded for long periods of time. But there are examples of successful collectives. The SEWA group of organisations started by Mrs Ela Bhatt and the AMUL pattern of milk cooperatives initiated by Dr Kurien are two examples of the successful collective organisations known all over the country. There are other organisations of marginalised groups in different parts of the country, some initiated by the producers themselves and others sponsored by civil society groups or the government.

All these groups exhibit some common features. The basic units of the successful collective entities are small homogeneous groups of members; there is a dedicated 'agency' to initiate and support them for a length of time; there are distinct gains in productivity and/or realisation of higher value for their products; and there is sufficient stress on capacity building. It needs to be emphasised that under present circumstances, homogeneous groups of small producers, with joint efforts to cater to their needs, will not only increase their bargaining power and income but also provide the foundation for an efficient and equitable rural structure. We have now sufficient experience of working with different models of collective organisations and should be able to adapt them to the given circumstances.

Exploiting the Market for Goods and Services: It was Dr Kurien's genius that he put market orientation of cooperative efforts at the central place. Both farm and non-farm producers in the rural economy have suffered because of faulty marketing systems. The gap between the prices received by the farmers and that paid by the final consumer is one of the most important indicators of its deficiency. This gap is not because of the value added at different stages of the marketing chain but largely because of leakages, wastage and high margins charged by the intermediaries. Such gaps are wider in the perishable products like fruit and vegetables, milk, and dairy products. The small farmers feel the incidence of market imperfection more seriously.

Initially the milk producers of Kaira district, and later dairy farmers all over the country who were members of the Anand pattern of dairy cooperatives, received a fair share in the consumers' rupee mainly because of astute marketing (which also included processing) by their cooperatives. For most of the farm produce, especially for the high-value products, aggregate demand is not a problem. With the burgeoning demand, the product mix and quality of the products on one hand and the marketing arrangements on the other have become very important for maximising producers' incomes. Reforms in marketing are as important as the investment in rural infrastructure. In fact, both can go together to enhance value of the produce and income of producers.

For non-farm products, especially those produced by the artisans in small enterprises, marketing is of paramount significance, not only for receiving signals regarding the effective demand for their products, but also for claiming a higher share in the consumer's spending. Today, the artisans and craftsmen are the most disadvantaged sections in rural areas because of the cheap products available from the urban organised sector due to easy accessibility exacerbated by inefficient marketing of their products.

For strengthening the market chain and making it more producer-friendly, government intervention is needed, particularly in strengthening marketing infrastructure. The producers also need to be trained to operate efficiently in today's more complex markets. This has become relatively easy with the spread of IT in the villages as that can reduce the information asymmetry, one of the principal causes of inefficient marketing. For small producers in the farm as well as non-farm sectors, marketing is an important element in what G.K. Prahalad in his seminal work, *The Fortune at the Bottom of the Pyramid*, has called "the ecosystem of wealth creation".

Development of Human Resources: Dr Kurien laid great emphasis on the development of human resources at all levels. The importance of human development as a measure of progress was recognised in our plans. 'Growth with justice' was a recurring theme in the Twelfth Plan with its emphasis on 'inclusive growth.' Of the three main components highlighted by United Nations Development Programmes' (UNDP) *Human Development Reports*, namely, income, education and health, I have already commented on the growth of income and status of poverty in rural areas. Let me say a few words on the other two major components of human development, namely education and health.

Education: Investment in creating educational facilities has increased phenomenally. As mentioned earlier, the infrastructure for education has been strengthened all over the country. This has brought about a profound change in the rural areas in terms of access to elementary, and to an extent secondary, and higher education. Yet several problems remain. There is a serious problem of 'exclusion' of weaker sections of society, particularly the SCs and STs, and minorities. There is a problem of dropouts with the retention period in schools limited to hardly three years. And above all, there is the problem of quality. Extensive surveys of rural educational institutions have shown that not only is the quality of teaching very low, there is also no sign of improvement. Further, in case of secondary and higher education, the students are not equipped for gainful employment. Skill deficit, which is common in the country, is more glaring in the rural areas. These problems have to be tackled to provide true benefits of the large and growing investment in education in the rural areas.

Health and Nutrition: The situation with regard to health and nutrition, another critical element of human development, is disappointing in the country; it is worse in the rural areas. We have not been able to meet the modest targets for reducing infant and maternal mortality set as part of the Millennium Development Goals (MDGs). As is well known, our record in correcting malnutrition is dismal. On all indicators of health and nutrition, the rural areas are far below the desirable norms. Investment in health infrastructure seems to be inadequate, even in comparison to some other developing countries. But it is not the only, or even primary, factor coming in the way of achieving satisfactory results. There seems to be some basic lacunae in designing of the projects and programmes, and more so in their delivery systems.

It is easy to explain failure of delivery due to inefficiency of the bureaucracy or imperfections of the market, but one wonders why, with the power given to *panchayats* to supervise various programmes of education and health, the situation has not changed. Explanation would go beyond economic logic. The nature of social organisations at the local level has to be understood and the scope for change has to be defined. For these purposes, academics and professionals can play an important role, as advocates as well as activists. Dr Kurien had visualised that role when he started the experiment of the Spear Head Teams for expanding the cooperative movement in the dairy sector. In this, as in several other aspects of rural development, there is much to be learned from the ideas and actions of this remarkable leader.

References

Chakrabarty, K.C. (2013). "Financial Inclusion in India: Journey So Far and Way Forward", *Reserve Bank of India Bulletin*. October.

Desai, Sonalde B., Amaresh Dubey, Brij Lal Joshi, Mitali Sen, Abusaleh Sharif and Reeve Vanneman (2010). *Human Development in India*. New Delhi: Oxford University Press.

Motiram, Sripad and Vamsi Vakulabharanam (2013). "Indian Inequality: Pattern and Changes, 1993-2010", in *India Development Report 2012-13*.

Mythili, G. and Nitin Hara (2013). "Sectoral Linkages, Multipliers and the Role of Agriculture", in *India Development Report 2012-13 (*edited by S. Mahendra Dev). New Delhi: Oxford University Presss.

Vyas, V.S. (2000). "The Second Round of Reforms in Agriculture", *Dantwala Memorial Lecture* delivered at the 83rd Conference of Indian Economic Association, January.

2

Challenge of Transforming Indian Agriculture*

Increased agricultural production in last 2-3 years cannot hide the fact that Indian agriculture is facing a serious crisis. The crisis is clearly evident in the falling share of agriculture in GDP (gross domestic product) with little decline in the workforce depending on agriculture; progressive diminution of agricultural holdings; and impoverishment of the large majority of farmers who cannot make two ends meet from their agriculture income. With 17 per cent share in GDP, agriculture is supporting nearly 52 per cent of country's workforce. A very large number of farmers, nearly 83 per cent, have holdings of less than 2 ha, and their number is increasing. Except in some special circumstances, e.g., the farmers growing vegetables or other high value crops, these holdings are economically non-viable.

As the farmers situation analysis revealed, most of the farmers have negative or, at best, a meagre income from agriculture. The challenge facing agriculture, and in a way for the economy as a whole, is to increase production on vast number of small agricultural holdings and enable a sizable number of workers to shift from agriculture to non-agricultural sectors. In most of the circumstances, increase in productivity in agriculture is a precondition for growth in the non-farm employment, particularly in rural areas. Hence I am concentrating on the factors that inhibit growth in productivity, and measures to overcome these inhibiting factors.

There is stagnation, if not decline, in yields of the major crops (Birthal *et al.*, 2014). Even in ancillary sectors such as dairy and

* Tarlok Singh Memorial Lecture delivered at Indian Association of Social Science Institutions (IASSI) Conference, Hyderabad, 14 October 2011.

horticulture, rate of growth is decelerating in the recent years. Need for major improvement in agricultural productivity is clearly indicated. With rising input costs and declining productivity, farmers' income is declining, resulting in acute distress. Near stagnation in agriculture is also affecting the consumers. While the demand for basic food as well as other agricultural products is increasing, especially after income-generating programmes for the poor such as Mahatma Gandhi National Rural Employment Guarantee Act (MGNREGA), the supplies are falling short, be it foodgrains, vegetables and fruits or animal husbandry products, thereby fuelling inflation.

Option of large-scale imports of foodgrains and other agricultural products is not realistic for our country. International prices of agricultural commodities are rising and are likely to continue the upward swing in next few years. An additional and complicating fact is that bulk of tradable surplus in important agricultural commodities such as rice and wheat is concentrated in two or three countries, making the price of these commodities largely dependent on the production in these countries, hence more volatile. More importantly, the income of a large section of workforce depending on agriculture can be sustained only if domestic production increases and terms of trade remain favourable. It should be recognised that in our situation, possibility of extending the area under crops does not exist. There is a clear need for a substantial breakthrough in agricultural productivity.

Vision of Dynamic Agriculture

It is important to be clear about the future of agriculture one is contemplating. We are envisaging a sector where increase in production is sustained by a class of economically viable small and medium farmers. This would necessitate transfer of a sizeable number of farmers with miniscule holding from agriculture to non-agricultural sectors. But this transformation will be predicated on a labour-intensive rural industrialisation in order to meet the demand generated by a productive farm sector. In other words, we are rejecting a scenario where small farms are amalgamated in large holdings supposedly to avail the economies of scale. We believe that the model is socially disruptive and economically inefficient. It is possible, as I will argue, to transform present agrarian structure from a stagnant and impoverishing one to a dynamic and just system.

Green Revolution: An Earlier Period of Growth in Productivity

We had gone through more or less similar period of stagnation in agriculture, especially in foodgrains production, in the mid-1960s when we were faced with a 'ship-to-mouth' situation, which threatened to compromise our political sovereignty. The country was saved due to the Green Revolution, which was characterised with significant enhancement in productivity. From the late 1960s to the middle of 1980s, agricultural production, especially of foodgrains, increased in a sizable way. The remarkable feature of agricultural growth in that period was doubling of agricultural output on virtually the same land area.

This was made possible, among other factors, because of a well-defined goal, namely food self-sufficiency. Political support, bureaucratic skills and scientific talents converged to achieve this goal. A variety of complementary measures were taken, such as development and extension of HYVs (high yielding varieties) of seeds, continued expansion of irrigation, and farmer-friendly price policies. Institutional support for research, extension, credit and marketing was provided to implement the yield augmenting strategy. Land reform legislation of the earlier period, though failed to achieve redistribution of land to any remarkable extent, did succeed in breaking the hegemony of large farmers and created conditions, which led to the emergence of a middle peasantry who spearheaded the Green Revolution. All this was achieved not due to a grand strategy, but by pragmatic steps in tune with the prevailing economic and political environment.

The strategy which made the Green Revolution a success had also inbuilt lacunae which became manifest over the period of time. Resting mainly on irrigated or well-watered land, it led to the neglect of rainfed area, and thus widened regional inequalities. Excessive use of chemical inputs resulted in deterioration of the quality of land and water. Heavy reliance on so-called superior cereals, i.e., wheat and rice, resulted in the neglect of more nutritious coarse grains. Price policy, which was designed to ensure adopters of the new technology that their cost of production would be recouped and at the same time ensured that gains of productivity would be shared between producers and consumers, became an *ad hoc* exercise to placate one or the other section. In any case, the input-intensive technology could not be sustained without huge food and input subsidies.

The Changed Circumstances

For forging a strategy with the objective of imparting dynamism to agriculture and ensuring improvements in the living standard of the households depending on agriculture, we have to appreciate the changes that have taken place in the sector and the country during the quarter of a century since the mid-1980s, i.e., in the post Green Revolution period. Agriculture today has become basically a small farm sector; its production base, land and water, is weakening; cropping mix as well as the demand pattern for agricultural produce is changing; it is much more integrated with other sectors of the country's economy as well as with external economies; there is technological fatigue especially in the crops grown in the rainfed areas; and there is a general decay in the self-help institutions. None of these can be ignored.

It is not that all the developments impinging on agriculture have been unfavourable. We have, for example, greater resources to invest in agriculture; developments of infrastructure in general and IT (information technology) in particular have helped not only in terms of better communication, but also in building greater awareness; private sector, which was always dominant in marketing, has now gained a significant presence in certain regions and for certain commodities in production processes with contract farming and through input delivery. Economic reforms in key sectors have resulted in improvement in terms of trade for agriculture, which has helped certain sections of cultivators in easier access to key inputs such as credit, and expanded the domestic as well as international markets for agricultural products. A few words on these major developments may be appropriate.

Indian agriculture is progressively becoming small farm agriculture. Dominance of small farmers was a major factor recorded since we started counting holdings under the Census of Agricultural Holdings and the National Sample Surveys (NSS). However, the phenomenon of large areas cultivated in the small and marginal holdings, now approaching more than 45 per cent of the total cultivated area in the country, has gone relatively unnoticed. Salient features of the existing agrarian structure can be briefly noted.

- For the country as a whole, small (including marginal) farmers constitute largest segment of agricultural holdings, with major concentration in Uttar Pradesh (UP), Bihar and Andhra Pradesh (AP).
- Practically in all states of the country, small holdings account for overwhelming majority of total holdings in the state. For the country as a whole, they account for 83.5 per cent of agricultural holdings.
- Share of land cultivated under these holdings in most of the states is one-third or more, of the total cultivated area, only exceptions are Maharashtra (31.7%), Punjab, (29.9%) and Rajasthan (22.6%). For the country as a whole, nearly 45 per cent of area is cultivated in the small holdings.
- Small farmers supply 62 per cent of paddy, 54 per cent of coarse cereals and 52 per cent of wheat.
- In most of the states, and in the country as a whole, the number of marginal cultivators and the area cultivated by them is progressively increasing.
- Only in a limited number of states, most notably in Punjab, both the number of small holdings and the area operated by them have decreased.

Above data pertain to the year 2003. As this process of diminution of the size of holdings continues, it should be factored in as an important element in the strategy for agricultural growth.

Another disturbing feature of agricultural growth in recent years is the stickiness of labour force. Share of GDP from agriculture in the total GDP is progressively declining, but there is no corresponding reduction in the workers depending on agriculture. In this context, another significant change is the progressive feminisation of agricultural labour force.

An equally important and worrisome fact is deterioration of the land resources. Although the estimates vary, it is generally agreed that one-third of the agricultural land is suffering from one or the other debilitating factor. Besides, the net area under cultivation, which has stagnated around 140 million ha, is likely to further diminish, as increasing pace of urbanisation and industrialisation will divert land from agriculture to non-agricultural purposes. Same is true for water. Claims of non-agricultural sectors on water are increasing, and efficiency in the use of water in agriculture is not improving. This is indicated by the fact that even with the expansion of irrigation, share of double-cropped area has not increased.

There is a significant change in the composition of agricultural produce. Now more than half of the value of agricultural produce is accounted by ancillary sectors such as horticulture, dairy and animal husbandry, and fishery. Within the crop sector also, major changes have taken place in the crop composition. Cereals are losing ground to so-called commercial crops. Within the cereal sector, superior cereals are gaining more land at the cost of coarse cereals, especially millets. Changing consumer preferences have triggered this change. With increase in income, importance of cereals, especially coarse cereals, is declining in consumers' food budget and share of expenditure on milk, fruits, vegetables, eggs and meat is rising. Producers are responding to these signals. Public distribution of food, through emphasis on wheat and rice in PDS (public distribution system), has accelerated this change.

Finally, agriculture is much more integrated with rest of the economy than was the case during the mid-1980s. There is integration both at the input end and at the production end. Share of purchased inputs in the input structure has gone up in a remarkable way. With the growing importance of horticulture, dairy and fishery sectors, more and more is being produced for the market. In the crop sector also, there is marked preference for high value crops. Changes in expenditure pattern—more expenditure on education and health thus necessitating cash income—have hastened this process of market orientation. As the number of marginal holdings is increasing and with that option of self-provisioning is weakening, this section also has to rely more on purchased food. With opening of the economy, foreign trade in agriculture, expressed as ratio of imports and exports to the gross value of agricultural produce, has risen. All these factors have made agriculture more market oriented and also highly sensitive to macroeconomic trends.

Indian agriculture is in a flux. We have seen that significant changes are taking place in its internal organisation as well as in the external environment. The policies and programmes should be designed while taking note of changes occuring in this sector, which are affecting lives of a large number of people. Agricultural transformation should aim, first and foremost, at improving income of the producers with enhancement in productivity.

Strategic Interventions

As mentioned above, one of the major handicaps faced by a large number of farmers is palpably small size of their holdings. Even with the gains in productivity, many of the miniscule-sized holdings will remain economically non-viable. In order to raise income of the bulk of agricultural producers, they should be enabled to have economies of scale in procuring inputs and selling their output. At the same time, providing opportunities to the small and marginal farmers for expansion of their holdings should be explored seriously. Let me touch upon the latter possibilities first.

Enlarging Small Holdings

Option of enlarging marginal holdings should not be ruled out. There are principally three ways in which the marginal farmers can be enabled to enlarge holdings: by stricter enforcement of existing ceiling legislation, by encouraging and legalising leasing-in of land, and by facilitating purchase of land by small farmers. None of these are impractical suggestions. These have been successfully tried out in different locations in the country. There is a need to scale up such initiatives.

Leasing Land

A large number of marginal and small farmers lease-in land to expand their meagre holdings. As most of the states have made tenancy illegal or much restricted, bulk of these transactions are not recorded. For example, NSS (2003) has recorded 7 per cent of the operated area as leased-in area and 11.5 per cent of rural households as those leasing-in land. Micro studies all over the country have shown that 15-35 per cent land is leased-in. Among the tenants, large majority are the marginal and small farmers. Only in highly commercialised areas, phenomenon of 'reverse tenancy' exists.[1] If tenancy can be made legal, within the provisions of ceilings legislation, and registered, more land, and on better terms, can be made available to the marginal and small farmers. It has been rightly suggested, "land lease markets are more flexible than land sales market and involve low transaction costs."

Redistribution of Surplus Land under Ceiling Legislation

The other major initiative for expanding the holdings, i.e., redistributive land reforms was tried in the past. The legislation provided for declaring ceiling on landholding and distributing 'surplus' land among landless, marginal and small farmers. This was a bold initiative, but proved to be totally flawed when it came to implementation. There were serious leakages at all stages: less land was declared surplus than what should have been declared (land declared surplus was hardly 2% of the cultivated area); less land was taken possession than the declared surplus; less land was allocated to the beneficiaries than was acquired; and less land was actually given for possession than what was allocated. Even then, as several micro-level studies have shown that where redistributive land reform could be implemented properly, those who got land did benefit. The Committee on State Agrarian Relations and the Unfinished Tasks in Land Reforms has suggested that substantial area of land can be acquired for redistribution, even if the existing laws on ceiling are properly implemented. One must agree, however, that in the given

1. I have discussed this phenonmenon long back in "Tenancy in Dynamic Areas", *EPW Review on Agriculture*, June 1970.

environment, redistributive land reforms are like "an idea whose days have gone."

Enlarging Holdings through Land Market

Resorting to market-led operations to enlarge holdings is not taken seriously in our country. This needs to be revisited.

True number of individuals who want to purchase land, as indicated by the bank credit advanced for the land purchase, has been negligible. At the same time, where ever the state took interest in acquiring land large chunks of land could be obtained. The cases of state acquiring land for establishment of SEZ (special economic zone) are fairly common. What is less known is the several initiatives of the states to acquire land for establishing homestead for landless rural households were also relatively successful. This route of expansion of marginal holdings should not be overlooked.

National Bank for Agricultural and Rural Development (NABARD) has a scheme to refinance amount advanced by the banks for land purchase, which was started towards the end of the year 2002. Hardly any state took advantage of the scheme; only Haryana showed some interest. There too, less than 8,000 persons availed of the scheme.

Reasons given for virtual failure of the scheme include:

- Information is not disseminated by the banks, or by the state governments in State Level Bankers Committee (SLBC).
- Land records have not been updated, hence banks find it difficult to advance loan.
- There is wide gap between District Land Ceiling Rates (DLC) and the market rates, small/marginal farmers are not in a position to fill the resource gap.
- Generally, the owners do not sell irrigated land, and there is little interest in purchasing small fragmented pieces of dry land.
- Large farmers are not interested in selling land as the land values are increasing rapidly.

All these hurdles can be removed, and an active land market can be brought to existence with benefits for the small farmers. But it will need active support of the state governments and the banks.

At least three states, Karnataka, Andhra Pradesh (AP) and West Bengal, acquired large areas of land for giving sites for home construction to the homeless people. The procedures evolved, especially in case of Karnataka, are a fair blend of market forces and state initiative. An active role has been given to *panchayats*. It should be possible to enlarge this programme to get land for the marginal farmers.

Improving Productivity on Small Farms

Other prong of the strategy is to improve productivity on farms, especially in the small farm sector. There was a good deal of research in 1960s and 1970s on the size-productivity relationship in agricultural sector. The overwhelming evidence suggested that the relationship was adverse and the small farms were more productive. The explanation given was that small farmers use their owned resources more intensively, resulting in higher productivity. The conclusion was challenged in the recent years as purchased inputs claimed larger share in the input structure and the small farmers were constrained as far as own cash resources, or credit, is concerned. But more recent evidence at the all-India level has suggested that per hectare value of output on the small farms is higher even today than that on the medium and large farms. It was ₹14,754 on the marginal farm and ₹13,001 on the small farms, as against ₹12,335 as average for all farms.

However, because of the small area, income generated by these households from agriculture is not adequate. Disadvantage of the small size is not compensated by higher per hectare output. It should be remembered that most of the south-eastern and eastern countries, including China, have smaller holdings than ours, yet mainly because of higher productivity, they are able to earn much larger income.

There is large scope to improve productivity and earn higher income from the traditional crops on the small holdings. Yields of these crops (i.e., rice, wheat, millets, etc.) are much lower than those obtained by the progressive farmers in the same regions. Possibilities of a remarkable increase in yield on all types of holdings are illustrated by the growth in area, and income from dynamic crops, such as Bt cotton, maize and soybean. The main features determining the growth of these crops are:

- size neutral, high yielding varieties;
- economy in input use;
- better quality;
- active participation of the private sector in input supplies, principally seeds; and
- growing market.

Such prospects exist in other major crops also (e.g., hybrid rice).

Shift to High Value Crops

Another option for the small farmers is to shift from low value subsistence crops to high value crops. As it is, typically a small farmer devotes some land and resources to high value crops to generate cash income. The share of the high value crop, such as spices, fruits and vegetables is slowly increasing. Logic for expansion of high value crops on small holdings is based on the following premises: increasing demand due to income growth and urbanisation; higher and regular income flow; and labour-intensive production.

With all these advantages, small farms find it difficult to make a major shift from grain-based cropping pattern to high value crops due to

- overarching requirement for self-provisioning;
- high capital requirement;
- difficulties in marketing; and
- high risks entailed in raising high value crops.

Of these handicaps, requirement for self-provisioning can be taken care of by an efficient PDS. Last three hurdles are more important.

Availability of Credit: There has been phenomenal growth in credit to agriculture from the organised banking sector in recent years. Yet the credit available to the small farmers is not increasing. Difficulties in availing credit are more severe for tenant farmers and those small farmers who are not able to offer collaterals. They have to depend on the informal sources to obtain credit on onerous terms. Innovations favouring small borrowers such as SHGs (self-help groups) have largely bypassed the small farmers, as the main thrust is on consumption loans, or loans to small artisans. Disintegration of cooperative credit system has further worsened their plight. A more focused attention is needed to provide credit to the small farmers, if they have to introduce high value crops on their holdings.

Marketing: Due to the small lot to sale, lack of holding capacity and immediate need for cash, small farmers are always at a disadvantage in dealing with the middlemen. These handicaps are aggravated in case of perishables like vegetable and fruits. For providing appropriate marketing facilities, along with transfer of superior technology and assured supply of inputs, contract farming is advocated. Contract farming is not a new innovation in Indian agriculture; it was introduced decades back by sugar factories both in the private and cooperative sectors, and later by milk unions. These arrangements were successful to the extent farmers had decisive voice in these institutions. Recent interest in contract farming by private sector should be encouraged. However, fair terms for contracting parties have to be ensured and an effective adjudication mechanism has to be established.

Risk Migration: Propagation of high value agriculture in Indian agricultural setting is predicated on the access to reliable instruments of crop and income insurance. Existing instruments such as agricultural crop insurance to mitigate weather-induced risks and MSPs (minimum support prices) to ensure minimum prices for the staple crops are not functioning properly. Defects in these devices are now well known and need to be corrected so that small farmers may take advantages of these protective measures.

Without proper and effective instruments of risk migration, to ask the small farmers to opt for high input-intensive, high-risk-prone, high value crops is to compound their difficulties. In the present circumstances, the better alternative will be to propagate mixed farming with emphasis on self-provisioning, and 'commercial crops,' or agriculture-related enterprises such as dairying, playing a supplementary role. This is the model which bulk of the farmers in risk-prone areas are adopting on their own.

With the existing institutional arrangements for risk mitigation and marketing, it will be advisable to stress upon strengthening of enterprises such are dairy: which ensure fuller use of small farmers resources; for which marketing facilities are reasonably well developed; and which are well accepted by this category of farmers.

The small farmers on the fringe of town who are growing fruits and vegetables should be supported to develop farm horticulture in a more efficient way. (However, with increase in demand for land in the periphery of towns and cities for housing and industrial use, comparative advantages enjoyed by the small farmers in, say, vegetable growing in the peri-urban areas are being threatened.) As a rule, for this highly vulnerable group, the strategy for diversification should be guided by the norm of 'from familiar to less familiar.'

Improvements in Delivery Systems

There are technologies available to raise productivity on the existing crops as well as to expand the share of high value crops. Policy environment at the macro level is by and large favourable. The major difficulty is the inefficiencies in delivery systems.

Whatever strategy is adopted, the success hinges on efficiency of the delivery systems. Bulk of the small farms are potentially viable in most of the ecological regions in our country provided institutional support is given to them in terms of extension, credit, and marketing and risk mitigation. An important ingredient of agricultural strategy should be to strengthen institutional structure so as to support the small farm agriculture. We have an extensive network of institutions, but they are of little avail to the small farmers.

Making Institutions Relevant to Existing Agrarian Structure

Strategy should be to adapt large delivery institutions in credit, input supply, etc., to the reality of small-scale agriculture by reducing transaction costs and protecting against high risk. This can be done as illustrated in the credit delivery by organisational innovations such as BC (business correspondent) model, and by use of IT and other technologies as practised by several private sector firms dealing in the agricultural input supply or marketing of agricultural produce.

For risk mitigation, there is a need for strengthening and improving existing crop insurance system, increasing the reach of the MSPs regime, popularising warehousing receipts as a negotiable instrument, aggregating farmers to operate in the future markets, and encouraging value chain financing by the financial institutions.

Reforming delivery systems in order to make them congruent to small farm agriculture is extremely important. State policies in this regard, as in other respects, should be consciously designed to support the small farm sector.

Aggregating Different Functions on Small Holdings

Policies for strengthening delivery system have to grapple with the main problem of higher transaction costs in order to deal with the small farmers, perceived higher risk in dealing with the small farmers, and limited capacity of the small farmers in absorbing high value inputs and credit. Solution to all these problems is some form of collective action.

We have tried with different forms of cooperative societies, from collective farming to different variants of joint farming societies, but these have not succeeded. But there are examples of successful cooperatives particularly in dairy and sugar sectors. Newer forms of aggregation for availing of inputs and marketing of produce, such as producers companies also have better record. For other types of collective actions, examples of several initiatives in AP (VELGU), Gujarat (SEVA) and Kerala (Kuttambshras) as well as of SHG federations in different parts of the country can be cited in this context.

There are certain features of successful group efforts, which need to be emphasised. The basic units in these structures are small, homogeneous groups of farmers; there is a dedicated 'agency' to initiate and support them for a length of time; there are distinct gains in productivity and/or realisation of higher value for their products; and there is sufficient stress on capacity building. We will like to highlight that in present circumstances, homogeneous groups of agricultural producers, with joint efforts to cater multiple needs of farming, can provide effective foundation for an efficient and equitable agrarian structure.

Integrating various functions such as input supply, extension and quality control, and more importantly, the marketing and processing with larger organisations in a vertical manner is another possible route. Even such arrangements will be more effective if farmer group srather than an individual farmer is a contracting party. We have now sufficient experience of working with different models of vertical linkages, and should be able to adapt them to the given circumstances.

We have successful examples of innovations supported by research and extension establishments, farmers organisations safeguarding and furthering members interests, innovative credit supply and marketing institutions, innovative risk-sharing arrangements, and successful interface with spot and forward markets by the farmers groups. But such examples are few and far between. India's vast small farm sector can be a strong feature of the economy, rather than a drag on it if such institutions and practices can be scaled up, and become the rule rather than exception.

Non-farm Employment

Main focus of my lecture today is the growth in productivity, particularly on the small farms. However, it is equally true that a large number of small farmers will have to shift from agriculture to non-agricultural sectors. If that has to occur due to the 'pull' factor of better opportunities, rather than the 'push' factor of lack of opportunities in agriculture, it will be important to understand what type of non-farm employment can be created and by whom. Such opportunities will be more sustainable if they meet the growing demands of a productive and prosperous agriculture. Since growth in the modern industries is virtually jobless growth, two principal avenues for non-farm employment will be wage-paid employment in programmes such as MGNREGA, and employment generated by rural industrialisation. There is enough written on employment schemes such as MGNREGA, hence, let me say a few words on rural industrialisation.

It is instructive to refer to China's experience in this regard. Agricultural prosperity in the earlier phase of reforms in China led to a spurt in household and prefecture level industries, in our terminology tiny and small industries. There were three main factors accounting for remarkable growth of rural industries in China in the initial phase of reforms. Firstly, these industries were geared to meet the requirements of small farms (machinery for small farms) and demand from prospering rural households (furniture, building materials). Secondly, rural entrepreneurs started them. Thirdly, they had excellent technical support by government programmes such as Spark programme.

These conditions can be fulfilled in our context too. Thanks to the reach of media and easy communication, Revolution of Rising Aspiration has also spread in the rural areas. With increased income, a vast majority of rural households will provide expanding markets for consumption and production-related goods. The large farmers in the country-side provide a pool of potential entrepreneurs who have investible resources, right contracts and capacity to bear risk—factors that are necessary to start and run a small enterprise. There is a network of institutions capable of transferring relevant technologies and imparting needed skills. We need a positive approach to rural industrialisation and give it an important place in plans and programmes.

Shift in Policy Stance

For ushering in a just and productive agriculture sector, we will also have to take careful look at the economic policies. One of the causalities of the 'economic reforms' is the neglect of agriculture in the policy domain. While formulating macro policies, agriculture is totally neglected. This is despite the fact that even with the declining share of GDP, agriculture remains the largest industry in terms of gross output. Of course, it is the largest employer in the economy. The major policy initiatives, be it in monetary policy, fiscal policy or trade policy, should be examined in reference to their impact on this large sector. This has become necessary as agriculture is getting more and more integrated not only with the domestic economy, but with global economies as well. Now it is deeply affected by macro policies.

Apart from macro policies, there is need to examine sector-specific policies also. Despite substantial reforms, there are still some kinks in the credit, marketing and trade policies. Price policies and trade policies are not properly aligned. Policy of 'cheap inputs-cheap outputs' implying huge subsidies needs to be reviewed. Greater attention has to be paid to the rural infrastructure in allocation of resources. Similarly, greater allocation has to be made for rejuvenating land and water resources, and on skill formation. Role of the private sector and of the public sector should be clearly defined in agricultural development. Above all, policies should recognise the reality of growing small farm sector.

We have to relate policies, programmes and delivery systems to the reality of a small-farm-dominated agrarian structure on one hand, and changing demand pattern for agricultural produce on the other. Then alone we will be able to face the challenge of transforming a stagnant and impoverishing agriculture to a just, efficient and dynamic sector.

3

Some Aspects of Structural Change in Indian Agriculture*

The agrarian system in a country reflects the main attributes of production units and their mutual alignment. These are not independent of each other, and factors influencing one aspect of the system affect other aspects as well. However, those favouring structural change stress upon changes in the relative position of different categories of agricultural producers as a pre-condition for changing the attributes of constituent units. It is understood that without appropriate supporting measures, gains from structural change can soon evaporate. Similarly, unless some vigour is imparted to non-agricultural activities, changes emanating from the agricultural ones cannot last long. The importance of generating and extending appropriate technology and measures to contend with demographic pressures is also realised in this context. While there is substantial agreement on these issues, there is not much clarity on the nature and magnitude of structural change witnessed during the last few years or the process by which such change could have come about.

In this paper, we will examine the changes in the structure of landholdings, an important, if not key, aspect of agrarian structure. The discussion will be carried out for the country as a whole and for major states. The period selected for this study is mid-1950s to early 1970s, although our major emphasis will be on the decade of 1960s. We will speculate on various processes by which the changes could have come about and the impact that such changes could have made on production level. We will conclude by underlining the need for a

---

* Presidential Address delivered at the 38th Annual Conference of the Indian Society of Agricultural Economics held under the auspices of the Assam Agricultural University, Jorhat, Assam, 18 January 1979.

proper alignment of institutional, technological and organisational factors in the context of the changed agrarian scene in the country.

I

Changes in the Size Pattern of Ownership Holdings

Production units in agriculture can be classified on the basis of size of landholdings, gross or net produce, value added, capital employed, extent of wage labour, extent of marketable surplus, gross or net worth of the enterprise, etc. As should be expected, Indian economists are not fully satisfied with a unidimensional measure of classifying production units in the agricultural sector. Holdings have been classified on the basis of area covered, gross product, gross and net worth, and extent of wage labour (Vyas, 1968; Rudra *et al.*, 1976; Patnaik, 1971). Yet, the predominant form of classifying production units is the size of landholdings expressed in acres (or hectares). This is partly because data on acreage of holdings are readily available and a whole set of information (land utilisation, cropping pattern, yield, etc.) is related to the size class of holdings thus defined.

Another reason for the bias towards the size of holdings in terms of acres is that, in Indian villages, control over land, and control and authority over local level institutions usually go together. Access to other factors of production in the villages is largely determined by the size of landholdings. In relatively homogeneous rural areas, even income differences among different households can be better explained by the size of landholdings than by other important variables (Repetto and Shah, 1975). Due to the overwhelming importance of land size, intervention in any scheme of structural reform in agriculture is sought, in the first instance, to affect the changes in the size pattern of landholdings.

By selecting acreage as the principal classifying element, comparability between different size classes of production units is not automatically ensured. The quality of land, tenurial arrangements and intensity of land use may differ significantly for different size-groups. These problems can be best tackled at the micro level of homogeneous region. However, due to paucity of data, in most of the cases, one cannot analyse the structural phenomena below the state level. Our analysis will also be based on state-level experiences. While taking the state as a unit for analysis, we are making two additional assumptions: (i) the land market is essentially confined within a state and (ii) inter-state rural migration is not significant.

Changes in Holding Pattern

The reports of various rounds of the National Sample Survey (NSS) are the principal source of obtaining an all-India picture of the distribution of landholdings. The landholding pattern in India has been investigated under three different rounds of NSS: 8th (pertaining to 1953-54), 17th (1961-62) and 26th (1971-72). For 1970-71, a census of holdings was also conducted as part of the world-wide Agricultural Census. The findings of the Agricultural Census, especially on the size of holdings, are not comparable with those of the NSS owing to differences in concepts and methodology (Sanyal, 1976). Partly for this reason and also because only the NSS provides broadly comparable information over a period of time, we have relied on the data collected in various rounds of the NSS for our study. Due to territorial reorganisation of the states and also minor changes in definitions, it is not possible to obtain three-point data for all states. In such cases, emphasis is laid on the comparison between the results of the 17th and 26th Rounds.[1] The period between the 8th and 17th Rounds is termed as phase 1; the period between the 17th and 26th Rounds is termed phase 2.

Table 3.1 gives the distribution of landholdings owned by households in 1953-54, 1960-61 and 1971-72 as revealed by the 8th, 17th and 26th Rounds.[2] One way to gauge the changes in the holding structure is to calculate the concentration ratios for distributions.

1. Comparison of the results of the 17th and 26th Rounds also causes some problems. For example, estimates of area owned for all states in the 26th Round are lower than that for the 17th Round. For the country as a whole, the estimates suggest a decline in area owned by nearly 7 per cent. In Bihar and Odisha, the measure of decline (-23.6% and -21.1% respectively) is such that the comparison of estimates warrants extreme caution. Estimates of operated area, though differing in the two rounds, are closer to each other for the country as a whole as well as for individual states.

2. In subsequent discussion, 'holdings' and 'households' are used synonymously. Since the proportion of jointly-owned holdings in the NSS sample was very small (Sanyal, 1976), such usage would not vitiate the results (see Sanyal, 1977).

The calculation of Gini coefficient for 1961-62 and 1971-72 shows that the landholding structure had become slightly less skewed (from 0.525 to 0.512)[3] by the end of the decade compared to the early years. However, the concentration ratio may conceal more than what it reveals. There are various ways in which the value of the concentration ratio may increase without in fact meaning an enlargement of bigger holdings at the cost of small-sized holdings. For example, medium sized holdings may expand in number and area at the cost of small and large holdings and may thus raise the coefficient of concentration. It will be necessary, therefore, to take a close look at actual changes in different size-groups of holdings.

To facilitate inter-class comparison, we have consolidated size-groups of holdings reported in the NSS rounds in five categories: marginal landowners (those owning less than one acre); small landowners (owning land between 1 and 5 acres); medium landowners (5-15 acres); big landowners (owing 15 to 50 acres); and large landowners (owing more than 50 acres of land). The following facts emerged from the study of data for the period 1953-54, 1961-62 and 1971-72 (see Table 3.1).

- The number as well as proportion of households in the marginal holding group has significantly increased.
- During the period 1961-62 to 1971-72, the acreage under marginal holdings has slightly declined.
- The number of small landowners has increased but their importance in terms of proportion of the total number of landowners has marginally declined.
- The area under smallholdings has increased both in acreage as well as in proportion to the total owned area in the country.
- In numbers, total area and per household area, medium-sized holdings displayed trends more or less similar to small-sized holdings.
- The number as well as proportion of big and large holdings

3. Gini coefficient can vary slightly depending on the exact formula used. In the above calculations, the formula used is that given by Kendall and Stuart (1963).

has declined, the only exception being a slight increase in the number of big farmers in 1961-62 compared to 1953-54.

- The acreage under large holdings has declined both in absolute terms and as a proportion of total acreage. This also holds true for big farmers, but for a marginal increase in acreage in 1961-62 compared to 1953-54.

II

Factors Underlying Structural Change

There are various ways by which shifts in the relative importance of different size-groups of holdings described above could have come about. There could be a 'ladder' process functioning in an upward or a downward direction. In the upward manifestation, it would mean landless workers acquiring land and become marginal landowners , who acquire more land and become small landowners, and small landowners by the same process emerging as medium landowners. The ladder can also work in the reverse direction when medium owners lose land and swell the ranks of small landowners, small owners are pushed to the marginal owner category, and marginal owners join the ranks of the landless. To compound the difficulties, positive effects of changes in ownership might be negated by those in the operational holding structure, or the latter may reinforce the former. In respect of structural change, the pattern of ownership has a greater significance. Hence in the subsequent discussion, we have mainly focused on changes in the ownership pattern.

It is interesting to note that, virtually in all states where we found bottom concentration, there was a decline in the number of non-owning households. This suggests that the phenomenon of landless acquiring tiny plots of land cannot be ruled out (Sanyal, 1977). At least, one carefully conducted study in Gujarat has concluded that there is some evidence, however, feeble, of a positive ladder from landless workers to small landowners stage (Desai, 1974). In the absence of similar studies for other parts of the country,[4] one can

4. There is a study focused on operational holdings in Haryana, which has concluded that small farmers were loser in terms of operated area (Bhalla, 1977).

examine a few relevant hypotheses with the help of aggregate data, an indirect evidence to explain the changes depicted in the preceding sections. As possible explanations, one can suggest: (i) purchase of land by marginal and small landowners and sale of land mainly by large and big owners; (ii) impact of land reforms and movements of similar nature like *bhoodan*, 'land-grab' etc., resulting in the breaking up of large holdings, and allocating land to small owners; and (iii) demographic pressure necessitating division of holdings. These could be identified respectively as market-induced, institutional and demographic processes.

Before discussing these processes, it needs to be emphasised that inter-class comparisons attempted above may conceal significant intra-class movements as well as information on 'entry' and 'exist' in different size-groups. Lack of relevant information precludes any systematic construction of a transition matrix. However, relative shift in the importance of different size-groups at two points of time as attempted above is an important indicator of structural change in the holding pattern.

Market Process

Even in developed countries, market transactions in agricultural land are not numerous. In traditional societies, such transactions are all the more limited because until a dire need arises, a peasant would not like to sell his land. Provisions of various legislations enacted in recent years also have contributed to the freezing of land market in India; for example, a ST (scheduled tribe) landowner cannot sell his land to a non-ST person. In spite of these factors, at least until the mid-1950s, there was some evidence of land being sold by small and medium landholders and purchased by large and absentee land lords (Rao, 1972). The classical pattern seemed to be indebtedness due to natural calamities or social ceremonies leading to hypothecation of land with moneylenders (who in many cases were big landowners) and eventual transfer of land to moneylenders or bigger landlords. During the 1960s, this process seems to have come to a halt. I have explained elsewhere the possible reasons for discontinuation of this pattern (Vyas, 1976). Briefly, the fear of ceiling legislation acted as a break to further expansion of the holdings of big and large farmers. Opportunities for further intensification of farming in several parts of the country lured cultivators with large liquid resources away from purchase of land. Tenancy legislations in a number of states made the process of buying land by erstwhile tenants easy; this process is well documented for the western region of the country (Dantwala and Shah, 1971). For similar developments in other parts, one has to rely on localised surveys and studies. Available evidence suggests that land market, tended to work in favour of small and marginal landowners rather than against them.

Institutional Changes

It would be wrong to assume that market forces alone, or in the main, were responsible for obtaining the results noted above. The land market was supplementing the efforts of land reforms which, played a much larger role in influencing ownership pattern. Directly, the imposition of ceiling on holding and allotment of surplus land among the landless led to diminution of bigger holding class and creation of small holdings. It is well-known, however, that direct transfer of land was not a quantitatively significant phenomenon, the total area of surplus land redistributed among the landless until the beginning of 1970s amounted to hardly one million acres. Only in a few states, legislative intervention, mainly ceiling legislation, did make remarkable impact on the size distribution of holdings, for example, in Jammu & Kashmir (J&K), Kerala and West Bengal. By and large, the indirect pressure exercised by legislation was more important. In spite of fictitious transfers and other devices employed by large landowners, enactment of land ceiling legislations led to large-scale disposal of land by big landowners, particularly absentee owners, to forestall the effects of legislation. Since tenancy legislation gave the right of purchase of land to the cultivating tenant, this process was further accentuated. However, the process did not unfold itself in a neat fashion. There were a large number of cases of ejection of small tenants as there were numerous cases of acquisition of land by the tenants. During the 1950s and 1960s, a remarkable shuffle took place in the countryside. It is yet to be fully documented, even though there is strong evidence to suggest that, in large parts of the country, small landowners and the landless were net gainers in this process. Small owners could retain their holding against the machination of larger farmers and they, as well as the landless, were the main beneficiaries once the larger farmers decided to dispose off part of their land to be on the right side of law. Movements such as *bhoodan* and 'land-grab,' though by themselves did not benefit the small and marginal farmers in a measurable way, did contribute in creating a climate such that the large farmers thought it wise to dispose off parts of their land. Factors that led to a diminution of holding size or encroachment of a poor farmer's land by the rich farmer proved to be weaker than those which were working in favour of small farmers or landless labourers (Vyas, 1962; Dantwala and Shah, 1971; Rao, 1972)

Demographic Pressures

While the increase in area under small holding groups (and retention of area in the marginal holding group) could be explained by market and institutional processes, the increase in their number is basically due to rising population in cultivating households and lack of alternative employment opportunities in the country size. An expansion of the household, or more commonly death of the head of the household, leads to division of holding among legal heirs. Unfortunately, there are no systematic studies of the household dynamics in the rural areas to arrive at a precise measure of sub-division of holdings over a period of time due to demographic factors. In the absence of such studies, one could only arrive at a rough approximation of changes in the number of agricultural holdings due to population pressure.

On the basis of what is decidedly a crude exercise, we have estimated the likely increase (from 1961 to 1971) in the number of holdings in different size-groups due to expansion in the number of households and partitioning of holdings, and arrived at the expected number of holdings and have them compared with the actual number as revealed in the 16th Round (Vyas, 1977). It was found that in the case of marginal holdings, the actual number of holdings was not more than the expected number of holdings. This means that a large number of new marginal holdings were created, apart from those which came about due to partitioning households. In other size-groups, the trend was just the opposite, suggesting net migration to other size-groups. The increase by demographic factors could be either by what we have described earlier as the reverse ladder process or by landless households acquiring small plots of land. From our discussion, the latter seems to be a more plausible explanation. Similarly, a reduction in the number of large and big holdings, could be due to either the migration of households, or more probably due to division of landholdings sliding them in the lower size-group. It bears repetition that the synoptic picture presented above conceals intra-size group changes; it also does not provide accurate description of the entry and exit from one size-group to other. Its chief merit is in presenting the final position after inter- and intra-size-group changes have been worked out.

IV

The Next Phase

Certain important conclusions follow from this review of structural changes in landholding pattern. It is suggested that, even in our present system, enough pressure could be generated by legislative and administrative processes enabling small farmers in the countryside to hold on their own. Impulses released by these reforms could be cumulative. The land market could be induced to function in a way beneficial to small and marginal farmers. The reform measure may also create a climate in which non-legislative redistributive movements could gather momentum.

But these rather favourable factors did not prove adequate for raising productivity, generating surpluses in agriculture, and triggering off a process of absorption of the additional workforce of small and marginal landholders in a gainful non-agricultural activities. While structural changes of the type described earlier were meant to help agricultural growth, the net outcome, judged in terms of production, was not at all satisfactory. The rate of growth in agricultural production was 3.6 per cent per annum during the 1950s, which came down to 2.2 per cent per annum in the 1960s. It is easy to summarise that the structural change we are advocating, i.e., a reduced skewness in holding pattern, is irrelevant; it could even be counter-productive. Both facts and logic go against this conclusion.

It will be instructive in this context to refer to the experience of some of the less developed over populated countries where redistributive land reforms were pursued with vigour. After careful examination of land reforms in various countries of Asia, the authors of the Second Asian Survey have concluded:

> Successful land reforms in the Republic of China (Taiwan) and Korea demonstrate that agricultural development can be achieved with a relatively even distribution of holdings of very small size. The redistribution of land seems to have enhanced the mobilisation of labour and rural savings in these countries, and undoubtedly raised the level of effective demand among the lower income groups who received the benefits of redistribution. These equity measures have tended to accelerate rather than impede economic growth (Asian Development Bank [ADB], 1977).

Nearer home, these findings are corroborated by a study jointly sponsored by Food and Agriculture Organization (FAO) and Indian Institute of Management, Ahmedabad. As a part of this study, district-wise data on production and productivity were collapsed in 57 agro-climatically homogeneous regions. Gini ratios were worked out for each of these regions. These ratios, along with per hectare application of fertilisers and proportion of irrigation, were regressed on the yield level of important commodities as well as aggregate agricultural output (per hectare) in each of the selected regions. Table 3.2 gives the results. It will be seen that the predictive value of the model is apparent only in the case of rice, sugar cane and aggregate output, where the value of R^2 is more than 0.5. In the first and last cases, Gini ratios are negatively and significantly related to the yield levels. It is not significantly related to the yield level of most of the other crops. The differing behaviour of rice and wheat yield levels in the face of structural inequalities are very significant. It suggests that if technology is as powerful as it happens to be in the case of wheat, structural inequalities probably do not matter significantly. Similarly, in commercial crops where per hectare paid-out costs are high, factors other than structural features—may be access to credit, or inputs, or marketing—are more important. In other cases, it appears that more equitable structure is an aid to higher productivity.

The results of the exercise also underline the importance of technical change. Although equitable distribution of holdings is likely to contribute to the level of production (per hectare) as is clear for rice as well as total agricultural output, the importance of technical change as embodied in fertiliser application and irrigation should be fully recognised. In fact, the relative importance of technical factors in enhancing levels of productivity is greater. Presumably, a more equitable distribution of land clears the deck for the application of superior technology.

In addition to the promise of productivity rise, more equitable distribution of holdings satisfies what Joshi (1975) has aptly described as 'equality urge.' It has far-reaching consequences. To quote him:

> In a traditionally hierarchical society which was founded on the principle of inequality the introduction of the concept of equality is revolutionary force challenging the entire ideological and institutional framework of social existence. It is the creator of new urges and aspirations among the have-nots and therefore the generator of social forces necessitating far-reaching innovations in the institutional patterns and paths of modernisation.... If the principle of equality—and equality also subsumes the elimination of the worst forms of social parasitism and poverty—has also to be a major premise of economic growth, it brings to the forefront the question of new institutional patterns contributing to the growth with equality (Joshi, 1975).

In countries where the notion of equality is translated in terms of more equitable access to land, the supportive institutions to agriculture are also favourably affected. Growth in modern agriculture crucially depends on various supportive measures, i.e., those related to research, extension, credit input, and product marketing. The extent of support received by the individual producer from organisations providing these inputs and facilities determines in a large measure his capacity to produce more. In the situation of unequal distribution of landholdings, the supportive systems are also geared to the demands of a relatively few resourceful holdings. On the other hand, in countries where a wider measure of equality in landholdings prevails, although holdings may be small, these very institutions get adjusted to the requirements of small holdings. To initiate the process of modernisation of agriculture may, therefore, suggest a larger emphasis on equitable distribution of holdings. In this respect, the changes in agrarian structure as witnessed during the last few decades are in the right direction, and if anything, they need to be further strengthened.

If what has happened over the period of the mid-1950s to early 1970s can be considered as a trend, and if the same trend can be projected for the next 20 years, it looks that by the end of 1980s, Indian farming will be basically characterised by medium and small holdings, and roughly three-fourth of the land will be cultivated in holdings below 15 acres, compared to less than half in mid-1950s. In some sense, the structure will be more equitable than what it was at the beginning of the planning era.

Already a sizeable class of middle peasantry has emerged in the country. The hegemony of large farmers in the rural areas is broken. The reduction in the skewness has had a favourable effect on both production and social environment. But in this process, small farmers have not materially benefited; at best, they have retained their share of land. Even after a break on the process of proletarianisation, the process of immoderation continues (Vyas, 1977). The conflict in the country has also shifted to that between the middle peasantry on one hand, and small and marginal farmers, on the other. Since the middle peasantry is not inconsequential in numbers and has strong links with other establishments, the conflict is becoming more pervasive and acute.

It is a moot question whether structural changes *per se* are likely to benefit the small farmers, or whether the solution to their problems lies in terms of an adaptive technology, supportive systems geared to their requirements, and most important, alternate or at least supplementary sources of employment. So far no effective dent has been made in these directions. Yet the emerging social conscience, new alignment of political forces and our better understanding of the operative systems should give us greater hope for evolving a viable strategy for small and marginal farmers.

Although the Indian experience in land reforms is important as it shows that the hegemony of large landholders can be challenged by a combination of legislative, market-induced and extra-constitutional moves, a different strategy is required to enable small and marginal farmers to consolidate their gains.

References

Asian Development Bank (1977). *Asian Agricultural Survey 1976: Rural Asia: Challenge and Opportunity*. New York: Praeger Publishers.

Bhalla, Sheila (1977). "Changes in Acreage and Tenure Structure of Landholdings in Haryana, 1962-72", *Economic and Political Weekly* XII(13), March 26.

Dantwala, M.L. and C.H. Shah (1971). *Evaluation of Land Reforms*. Vol. I. Bombay: University of Bombay.

Desai, M.B. (1974). "Changing Farm Production and Organisation in Surat", *Mimeo*. Baroda: M.S. University of Baroda.

Joshi, P.C. (1975). "Land Reforms: A Trend Report", in *A Survey of Research in Economics*. Vol. IV–Agriculture, Part II. Bombay: Allied Publishers Pvt. Ltd.

Kendall, M.G. and A. Stuart (1963). *Advanced Theory of Statistics*, Vol. I. London: Charles Griffin and Co. Ltd., p. 46.

Patnaik, Utsa (1971). "Capitalistic Development in Agriculture: A Note", *Economic and Political Weekly* VI(39). September 25.

Rao, V.M. (1972). "Land Transfers in Rural Communities: Some Findings in Ryotwari Region", *Economic and Political Weekly* VII(4), September.

Repetto, R. and Vimal Shah (1975). "Internal Policies for Income Redistribution: A Case Study in Rural India", *Occasional Paper* No. 2. Ahmedabad: Gujarat Institute of Area Planning.

Rudra, Ashok, A. Majid and B.D. Talib (1969). "Big Farmers of Punjab", *Economic and Political Weekly* IV(39). September 27.

Sanyal, S.K. (1976). "A Review of the Conceptual Framework of Landholdings Survey", *Indian Journal of Agricultural Economics* XXXI(3). July-September.

———. (1977). "Trends in Some Characteristics of Landholdings: An Analysis for a Few States", *Sarvekshana* I(1 & 2), July and October.

Vyas, V.S. (1962). "Land Reforms in India: Review of a Decade", in M.R. Sinha (ed.), *A Decade of Economic Development and Planning in India*. Bombay: Asian Studies Press.

———. (1968). "Economic Efficiency on Small Farms of Central Gujarat", in *Seminar Series-VII*. Bombay: Indian Society of Agricultural Economics.

———. (1976). "Structural Change in Agriculture and the Small Farm Sector", *Economic and Political Weekly* XI(1 & 2). January 10.

———. (1977). "Mainsprings of Agricultural Growth in India", *Panse Memorial Lecture*. New Delhi. August 9.

Table 3.1

Estimated Number of Households and Area Owned by Different Size-Group of Holdings (All-India)

Size-group of ownership holdings	*Number of Households and Area Owned (in '000)*								
	1953-54			*1961-62*			*1971-72*		
	No. of Households	*Area Owned (acres)*	*Average Area (acres)*	*No. of Households*	*Area Owned (acres)*	*Average Area (acres)*	*No. of Households*	*Area Owned (acres)*	*Average Area (acres)*
Marginal (below 1 acre)	15,360 (31.43)	4,166 (1.36)	0.27	23,579 (36.84)	5,062 (1.59)	0.21	35,640 (43.99)	4,910 (1.58)	0.14
Small (1-4.99)	17,448 (35.71)	45,670 (14.95)	2.62	22,468 (35.11)	58,465 (18.39)	2.60	27,415 (33.84)	71,158 (22.86)	2.60
Medium (5-14.99)	11,145 (22.81)	95,230 (31.18)	8.54	13,002 (20.32)	109,703 (34.52)	8.44	13,564 (16.74)	112,464 (36.13)	8.29
Big (15-49.99)	4,306 (8.81)	106,795 (34.97)	24.80	4,514 (7.05)	109,252 (34.37)	24.20	4,058 (5.01)	96,856 (31.12)	23.87
Large (50 and above)	604 (1.24)	53,580 (17.54)	88.71	437 (0.68)	35,379 (11.13)	80.96	350 (0.43)	25,856 (8.31)	73.87
Total	48,863 (100.00)	305,441 (100.00)	6.25	64,000 (100.00)	317,861 (100.00)	4.97	81,027 (100.00)	311,245 (100.00)	3.84

Note: Figures in parentheses are percentages to the total.

Source: NSS No. 36, 8th Round for 1953-54, NSS No. 144, 17th Round for 1961-62, and NSS No. 215, 26th Round for 1971-72, Tables on Land Holdings Cabinet Secretariat. Government of India.

Table 3.2

Yield Regression for All India (1971-72)

Crop yields	*Functional Form*	*Coefficients For*			*Constant*	*D*	*R^2*	*F*	*df2*
		X_1	X_2	X_3					
Rice	L	18.40	819.42	–883.02	1186.53	–	-518	17.17	48
		(4.14)*	(2.66)**	(–1.32)***	(3.24)*				
Wheat	L	4.69	1159.00	–366.54	1077.65	–	-171	3,24**	47
Bajra	L	5.23	345.86	–67.58	436.00	–	.359	6.16*	33
		(1.36)***	(1.33)***	(–0.14)	(1.64)***				
Jowar	L	15.41	–154.28	–1061.70	975.74	–	.288	4.85*	36
		(3.28)*	(0.51)	(–1.82)	(3.05)*				
Maize	DL	0.28	–0.09	5.87	–	.196	3.51**	43	
		(3.08)	(–1.15)	(12.52)*					
Cotton	L	–0.05	193.27	176.13	–6.48	–	296	4.35*	31
		(–0.03)	(1.85)**	(0.85)	(–0.05)				
Groundnut	L	5.90	81.62	567.96)	282.07	–	.225	3.38**	35
		(1.05)	(0.25)	(0.85)	(0.78)				
Rapeseed and Mustard	DL	0.005	0.16	–0.57	6.04	–	.315	4.29**	28
		(0.07)	(2.54)*	(–1.70)**	(17.50)*				
Sugarcane	DL	0.12	0.04	–0.16	7.92	0.52	.651	22.42*	48
		(2.93)*	(0.99)	(–0.57)	(32.84)*	(7.40)*			
Aggregate Agricultural Output	L	22.71	440.99	–907.78	1140.00	–	.627	24.64	44
		(5.89)*	(1.59)***	(–1.37)***	(3.15)*				

Note : Figure in parentheses are L values.

1. Except for aggregate agricultural output, all crop yields are in kilograms per hectare. Aggregate agricultural output of a given crop is evaluated at the same price to eliminate variation due to price differences in various regions.
2. Those regions in which the concerned crop did not have a significant place were dropped.

* Significant at 1 per cent. ** Significant at 5 per cent. *** Significant at 10 per cent

L = linear; DL = double log.

X_1= Fertiliser (kg per hectare of gross cropped area).

X_2 = Irrigation ratio (ratio of gross irrigated area to gross cropped area).

X_3 = Gini ratio of distribution of owned land.

D = Dummy for region; taking the value of 0 for north and northeast regions and l for the other regions.

4

Structural Change in Agriculture and the Small Farm Sector in Gujarat*

I

A comparison of the population census data for 1961 and 1971 reveals certain disquieting features. In the rural workforce in India, the number of cultivators and 'other workers' (artisan, etc.) has decreased, while that of agricultural labourers has significantly increased. Barring a few states, all states seem to have witnessed this development. In particular, the increase in the number of agricultural workers is a feature which is observed in every state. Since the total number of rural workers reported in 1971 was slightly smaller than in 1961, changes in different categories of workers emerge more sharply in percentage terms (see Appendix A-4.1).

An analysis of the distribution of workforce over the two census years is, however, risky because of the changes in the definition of 'workers.' Available data cannot overcome these definitional hurdles, and one will have to wait for the promised tabulation of 'non-workers' by secondary activity to attempt any worthwhile exercise in comparing changes in the total workforce over the years. It is reported, however, that the definitional changes would not have significantly affected the category of male workers (Krishnamurthy, 1972). Assuming that the male-female proportion in the rural workforce has remained the same over the decade, male workers can be used as a proxy for the total workforce. Even so, the results are not materially different. In

* Presidential address delivered at the 7th Gujarat Economic Conference held at Valsad under the auspices of Shri Nootan Kelvani Mandal, 15-16 November 1975.

the male workforce, there is a slight decline in the number of other workers, a marginal increase in the number of cultivators, and a sharp increase in the number of agricultural workers. Again, the picture is more vivid in percentage terms (see Appendix A-4.1).

A highly significant rise in the number of agricultural workers and, more importantly, a rise in the proportion of agricultural workers in the rural workforce has prompted some scholars to conclude that the process of proletarianisation in the rural areas is going apace. According to them the small farmers are losing their land and are swelling the ranks of the agricultural workers. The process of decay of cottage and household industries and the recourse of artisans and craftsmen to agricultural labour is also a part of the same scheme of things. This process is a continuing one; the changes recorded in 1971 began decades back. It is maintained that this process can be best described in terms of the dialectics of capitalist development in rural areas.

A few scholars well versed in Marxian lore have brought forth highly subtle, if not esoteric, arguments to support their theses, which in turn are refuted by more subtle and still more rarified arguments by equally renowned scholars. I do not claim that I understand all the refinements and subtleties of the *shastrartha*—this debate. However, the burden of the song seems to be that a process of proletarianisation, analogous to the process witnessed in the non-agricultural sector, is operating in the rural areas. The nature of expropriation may not, necessarily, be evidenced in an increase in the size of holdings of the larger farmers; it may be reflected, as the classical English pattern established, in more capital-intensive agriculture. Yet its final outcome would be, it is maintained, the ejectment of small farmers from land and the incorporation of their lands in larger farms. There may be certain deviations from the general rule that 'the big fish eats the small fish.' For example, in many areas, the medium-sized farmers, instead of the large farmers, are in the vanguard of the new, capital-intensive technology. They, rather than the larger farmers, have assumed the role of capitalist farmers. This can, however, be treated as a special case, rather than as an exception and much less as a negation of the above-stated principle. The process of concentration of gains in fewer hands, pauperisation of larger sections of the peasantry, and their eventual eviction from land could still continue unabated.

More fundamental questions would be: Are small farmers selling off (or leasing out) their land and are these lands bought (or leased in) by large or medium-sized farmers? Are such transactions taking place on a scale that would possibly lead to a transformation of the holding pattern in agricultural land within a few years? Are the ranks of agricultural workers swelled by the expropriated peasantry?

These questions cannot be fully answered only with the help of the population data; they would require an examination of the changes in the pattern of agricultural holdings over a period of time. More important, the answers to such questions pre-suppose an understanding of the dynamics of rural development in the context of overall developments in the economy, the society and the polity.

It will be my endeavour to examine some of these questions in the context of the rural economy of Gujarat. The imposition of this restriction on the analysis, i.e., examining a phenomenon as it manifests itself within a region of a large country, has its advantages as well as disadvantages. But let me state at the outset that my choice is dictated mainly by a slightly better familiarity with the rural economy of Gujarat rather than by any methodological consideration.

To begin with, one may observe that some of the scholars commenting on the pattern of change in rural areas have not maintained the distinction between agricultural holdings and cultivating workers (or cultivators). Thus, more than one worker may be wholly or partly dependent on a holding, which is generally coterminous with a household, even though all of them may not be working on the holding fully or even partly. An increase in the number of agricultural labourers does not, therefore, necessarily mean a reduction in the number of agricultural holdings. To judge what has happened to the holding pattern, we will have to look into some representative sample surveys or censuses of holdings over a period of time.

There are two main sources of information on the distribution of agricultural holdings in Gujarat: the National Sample Surveys (NSS) and the Agricultural Census. The Agricultural Census data pertain to one point of time, i.e., 1970-71. On the other hand, two NSS studies (Round 16 and Round 26) had examined the size distribution of holdings with a gap of a decade, in 1960-61 and in 1970-71. Hence, with NSS data, a two-point comparison is possible. The comparison of results of the NSS Rounds 16 and 26 yields certain significant conclusions. These are:

- The share of large holdings, i.e., holdings with 25 acres and more, has declined in terms of area as well as number.
- The share of medium-sized holdings, say 5-25 acres, has remained more or less constant in terms of area cultivated, although their share in total number of holdings has declined.
- The share of small holdings, i.e., upto 5 acres, has increased in terms of both the total number of holdings and the total number of cultivated area though there is no perceptible change in average size of the holdings (see Appendix A-4.2).

These are very significant results. They give an indication of the nature of structural change taking place in Gujarat's agriculture. The decline in the importance of large farmers, both in terms of number and the area cultivated, and the stability in average area of the holdings of small farmers is of particular significance, although until we have some more knowledge about the 'entry' and 'exit' in different holding-size categories, the exact implications of these findings cannot be determined accurately. It is quite possible that a certain number of medium-sized farmers might have lost land and come into the small farmers' category, while a balancing number of small farmers might have lost land and become sub-marginal cultivators or landless labourers, and both movements might have balanced each other. What happened in different categories of farms *inter se* cannot be judged from the aggregate data. For this, we need some more information on the process of change in the countryside. This can only be provided by detailed micro-studies.

In Gujarat, fortunately, we have a few well-conducted regional studies covering a fairly large span to time. The Resurvey of Matar Talukas by Vimal Shah and C.H. Shah covers 25 years, from 1929-30 to 1965-66. The study made by M.B. Desai and his colleagues, "Changing

Farm Production and Organisation in Surat", covers a period of five year from 1967 to 1971. M.L. Dantwala and C.H. Shah's "Evaluation of Land Reforms" looks into landholding data for almost a decade (1956-57 to 1964-65) in the selected villages of three districts of Maharashtra and Gujarat. The Gujarat survey was located in selected villages of the two talukas of Nadiad and Matar of the Kaira District. These studies differ in the period covered in their primary objectives, and in the methodologies adopted by the authors. All these, however, merit a close look by students of structural change in rural Gujarat.

Even at the cost of the exactness of the original studies, we may generalise certain basic conclusions of these studies. The common findings of these studies are:

- The importance of large farmers is declining in Gujarat's agriculture. In terms of both the absolute number and as proportion of the total holdings, the fall is clearly evident.
- The importance of medium-sized farms has remained unchanged.
- The number and proportion of small farmers is increasing, but so also, it seems, is the land they cultivate, thus making average size of the holding in this category virtually the same or slightly larger. (Only M.B. Desai's study has reported a slightly diminution in the average size of the holding of small farmers.)

These conclusions are consistent with the those reached earlier with the help of the NSS data at the state level.

Now, if one were to reconcile the fact of a sizeable increase in the number and proportion of agricultural labourers with the above quoted findings, the explanation could be sought in one or more of the following:

- The swelling in the ranks of agricultural workers could be due to a natural increase in the population of labourers' households and the lack of alternative employment opportunities for them.
- The increase in the number of agricultural workers would be due to an influx of the dispossessed small farmers.

- The increase in the number of agricultural labourers could result from the fact that additional workers in small farmers households could not get adequate employment on own farms.
- The increase could also be due to the fact that artisans and other workers did not get enough employment in their traditional occupations and therefore joined the ranks of the agricultural workers.

The studies quoted above lend support to all these propositions, but they also reveal that the relative importance of various explanatory factors differs significantly. For example, the aggregate data as well as the micro studies clearly bring out the lack of diversification in the rural economy. They also point out that the outmigration from agricultural labourers' household could ease the pressures only to a limited extent. But rise in the number of agricultural labour is of an order which cannot be explained solely by an increase in the population of agricultural labourers' households. Clearly, the ranks of the agricultural labour have swelled with an influx from some other categories of the rural workforce.

A convenient explanation for this increase in the agriculture labour force would be the dispossession of land of small farmers, what we had referred to above as the process of proletarianisation. None of the studies reveal any sizeable dispossession of land of small farmers. The Surat survey does report shedding of land of small farmers (up to 5 acres) and large farmers (over 25 acres), but the total land disposed off as compared with the area under each holding size category is negligible. The Matar resurvey reports that between 1929-30 and 1965-66, the large holders of land in the Matar taluka in net lost some land which was acquired by the small- and medium-sized farmers, although the size of land thus transferred was small.

Dantwala and Shah's study is more pertinent in this connection as they directly pose the question of 'arrivals to' and 'departure from' different size-groups of holdings. In the first place, they confirm the hypothesis that there were few market transactions in land since the mid-1950. Most of the changes in landholdings were due to land reform legislation. Thus, in the two talukas surveyed by them, a large majority of the farm families (85% in Nadiad and 71% in Matar) remained in the same size-group over the entire period, even though the period covered by them was one of great shuffle in the countryside.

The most striking finding of the study is that out of the total 'arrivals' into the small farm category, a large majority came from below, i.e., the phenomenon of landless farmers acquiring land was much more prominent than that of small farmers losing land and becoming landless farmers (see Appendix A-4.2). It should be remembered that the study was done in the context of the Tenancy Legislation of Gujarat, which aimed at giving ownership rights to the erstwhile tenants who were the actual tillers of land. The study clearly establishes that landless labourers cultivating land on lease and small tenant farmers were benefited by the legislation. Even if it is assumed that the picture obtained by this study reflects the initial reaction to the legislation affecting the very basis of the relationship in land and that this cannot be considered as a normal occurrence in the countryside, it does cast serious doubts on the hypothesis of proletarianisation of the small peasantry in the 1950s and 1960s.

It is really the third and fourth possibilities, namely, the influx of surplus members from the small farmers' households and of artisans and other workers in rural areas, which can explain bulk of the increase in the proportion of agricultural labourers in the rural workforce. The process of surplus workers from the small farmers' households joining the agricultural labour force is graphically described in the Matar resurvey. I cannot do better than quote from this study.

> The constancy of the unchanging structure (of holding) conceals the process of continuous afflux of a section of landholders into the category of landless workers. The total population increased by about 100 per cent between 1929-30 and 1965-66. Such a large increase in the average size of the family and in total population consists partly an increase in size of family and partly in the total number of families. Taking families in all occupation groups, we find that the average size of the family had increased from 4.8 persons in 1929-30 to 5.4 persons in 1965-66 or by about 12.5 per cent. Taking cultivators, we find that the size of family for their group also increased by 20 percent. The average landholding per capita declined only marginally from 0.92 acres to 0.90 acres. The bulk of the increase in the number of persons that belong to the erstwhile families of landholders would have been deprived of their land, they might

have become landless. This is supported by the fact that the proportion of agricultural labourers which was 14.8 per cent in 1911 and 17.2 per cent in 1921 jumped to 26 per cent 1961 (Shah and Shah, 1974).

Finally, the role of artisans and other workers in rural areas in swelling the number of agricultural labourers needs to be emphasised. Macro-level surveys as well as micro-level studies clearly bring out the fact that the number of artisans and other workers is progressively dwindling and that they are joining the agricultural labour force in large numbers.

Thus enough empirical evidence exists to support the hypotheses that has been put forward to explain increase in the number of agricultural labourers in the rural areas of Gujarat. Another possibility which is based more on inference than on direct evidence can be suggested. There is a strong possibility that a large number of workers who report themselves as agricultural labourers do so not because they have no land to cultivate, but because that land may not supply them with the wherewithal for living even at the subsistence plane, and thus they might have been forced to take recourse to agricultural labour as the principal source of earning. In other words, a large number of the agricultural labourers may still have some claim on land. Before we dwell on this aspect and see its wider implications, it bears repetition that for the recent years, there is no evidence of large-scale ejectment of small farmers by the larger farmers and although the phenomenon of proletarianisation of small peasantry may be a distinct possibility, it is not an immediate reality in Gujarat. The facts support the hypothesis that a hard core of the small farm sector has come to stay in Gujarat's agriculture.

II

If the lack of evidence on large-scale eviction of the small farmers does not fit in with the model of structural change propounded by some Marxian scholars, the data on the low level of efficiency in the small farms will not give comfort to economists of the neo-classical school, some of whom have made a fetish of the high (per hectare) efficiency on small farms.

For discussing the level of efficiency obtained in various categories of farms, we will take recourse to the earlier cited studies and a similar taluka-wide study of the Borsad taluka of the Kaira District conducted by the Agro-Economic Research Centre of the Sardar Patel University (Bhat, 1960). Over and above these, two more sources can be utilised. The Agricultural Census conducted in 1970-71 throws valuable light on the agrarian economy of the state. Unfortunately, so far, even after a lapse of four years, only a few statements based on the census are available in published form.[1] Recently, the Reserve Bank of India (RBI) has published some results from the All-India Debt and Investment Survey of 1971-72.[2] In this case, also so far, only details of the assets and liabilities of rural households are published.

Before we present some of the results from these studies, it may be considered necessary to make the ritual disclaimer on suitability of the size of landholdings as a measure to judge the efficiency on now familiar grounds, i.e., land is one of the several inputs, its importance is declining and the 'inherent' characteristics of soil differ from one site to another. One may question that if land is just one and a progressively less important factor of production, why the inherent characteristics—except in extreme cases like arid or saline or rocky lands—should matter?

The answer to this question is relevant for our discussion. Although our primary focus is on the changes in the size distribution of landholdings, what we are aiming at is to ascertain the income-earning capacity of holdings of different sizes. The comparison among different categories of holding from this point of view would be invalid only if the lands are situated in different agro-climatic zones, cultivated under significantly different institutional arrangements and serviced by vastly different infrastructure. As we are making comparisons between size groups of holdings within selected talukas, the factors cited above should not be varying as to invalidate the results. Most of the factors, like intensity in the use of inputs, which are given as

1. These statements are reproduced in *Socio-Economic Review, Gujarat State, 1974-75*, Ahmedabad: Bureau of Economics and Statistics, Government of Gujarat, 1975..

2. *All-India Debt and Investment Survey, 1971-72, Vol. II: Assets and Liabilities of Rural Households as on 30th June 1971*, Statistical Tables, All-India and States, Bombay: Reserve Bank of India, 1975.

the determining variables as far as farm productivity is concerned, are in essence reflections of a given distribution of landholdings, and the factors and product markets that have emerged largely due to such a distribution. The size of the landholding is an index, and in most circumstances a sensitive index, of the economic handicaps or advantages faced by various groups of cultivators in an area. There is much to commend in the traditional wisdom, which equate small farms with handicapped farms.[3]

In the mid-1950s and the early 1960s, the dominant view among Indian economists was that small farms were more productive, on the per hectare basis than large farms. Highly ingenious explanations were offered to prove the supposed efficiency of the small farms.[4] I had expressed some doubts on this inference.[5] The evidence available since then further corroborates the view that in terms of per hectare income, small farms are at a disadvantage.

Unfortunately, not in all the studies cited earlier the information is organised in a manner to enable one to examine the per hectare income on different size categories of farms. Yet two of the regional studies provide enough evidence to support the above-stated view. The Matar resurvey and the Surat study have concentrated more on the per hectare gross value of output on farms of different sizes. Both these studies have shown that the per hectare value of output is the lowest on small farms. This could be due to either one or both of the following reasons: (a) small farms might be growing low value crops and (b) yield per hectare of the crops grown may be low. As it happens, both the factors operate on small farms.

For the cropping pattern on farms of different sizes, we have state-level data from the Agricultural Census of 1970-71. Considering the state as a whole, hardly 55.3 per cent of the cropped area was under foodgrains; this percentage varied from 79.0 to 67.2 on small farms

3. A more sophisticated exercise by Vimal Shah and G. Repetto has shown that the bulk of the income inequality in rural areas of Matar could be explained by the ownership of land. The variables considered by the authors were (1) physical capital, (2) human capital, and (3) labour resources, see Shah and Repetto (1975).

4. For a review of this discussion, see Saini (1971).

5. See Vyas (1968).

(below 0.5 to 2 ha). The area under high value commercial crops like groundnut, cotton or tobacco was correspondingly low on these farms (see Appendix A-4.3).

The yield data, which are available only from the regional surveys, clearly shows that, by and large, the per hectare yield of all crops is lower on small farms. The difference in the yield level on large and small farms is all the greater in the case of commercial crops.[6]

A more meaningful comparison would be the per hectare net income on farms of different sizes after deducting all the costs, Cost C in farm management terminology. Such information is readily available only from the Borsad survey. In most other cases, the income is determined by deducting, largely, the paid-out cost, or the Cost A2 as it has come to be known in farm management parlance. On the basis of the retabulated data, I had reported earlier that the input-output ratio, on the basis of Cost A2, worked out to be slightly in favour of small farms: 2.68 on small farms (0.01 to 2 ha) as compared with 2.53 on large farms (5.01 to 15 ha). On the basis of Cost C, the ratios were 1.66 and 1.72 for small and large farms respectively (Vyas, 1968: 74). In other words, it is not because of the greater efficiency on small farms, but because of the fact that a significant item, family labour, is not taken into account, that the input-output ratio seems to be favourable on these farms.

The narrow base of the production activity, and the proportionately lower returns on this base, has given rise to what may be called, the phenomenon of immiseration, that of increasing destitution. One way in which this phenomenon operates is a growing reliance of the small farmers' households on wage-paid agricultural labour. The other way in which it manifests itself is the lack of investment on land to improve, or even to retain, its productivity. The tendency to grow low value crops which are normally correlated with a limited use of purchased inputs, is another symptom of this malady.

6. See M.B. Desai, Surat Study, pp.159-62. The results of Borsad Survey as retabulated by V.S. Vyas showed that for wheat and bajra, small farmers had more or less the same yield rates as large farmers, but for tobacco (the principal commercial crop of the area) and also paddy, yields on small farms were significantly lower (Vyas, 1968: 74).

We have already commented on the preponderance of low value subsistence crops on small farms. There is ample evidence to prove that on these farms most of these crops are grown with owned resources; the share of purchased inputs in general and modern inputs in particular in the cost structure is only marginal. The most important among the modern inputs is fertilisers. The Surat study shows that during the four years from 1968-69 to 1970-71, the use of fertilisers on small farms (on a per acre basis) was between one-fourth and one-fifth of the average per acre use of fertiliser on all farms in the area. (The highest per acre use was on medium-sized farms, i.e., on farms between 5 and 15 acres in size).[7] The use of other modern inputs on small farms was even lower. It is worthwhile to reproduce the conclusions of the Matar survey in this connection.

> More than the yields the difference in the levels of efficiency between the small farmers and other groups can be seen from the analysis of the use of resources. The difference arises mainly in regard to the use of inputs like irrigation, fertilisers. For instance, in regard to irrigation an input known to farmers vital differences were observed. Farmers with 10 to 25 acres had nearly two-fifths of the total area under irrigation against under 30 per cent of the cultivated area under irrigation on small farms. Expenditure for manures was more or less the same for big and small farms in 1929-30; in 1965-66, the big farmers spent nearly 50 per cent more per acre than the small farmers did for purchasing fertilisers from outside. The use of improved varieties also showed a similar difference between the small farmers and other groups. In regard to paddy, the small farmers grew predominantly an inferior variety Sutarsal (45 per cent of the area), compared to Jirsal an improved variety (87 per cent of the area) grown by the big farmers (Shah and Shah, 1974: 26).

In this context, a word on irrigation may not be out of place. In large parts of India, irrigation is rightly considered a crucial input for agricultural growth and stability. Its role in enhancing productivity significantly, more so as a precursor of other modern inputs, and its risk minimising value are well recognised. There is a general impression that proportionately more area of land of the small farmers is under irrigation. This has significantly contributed to the belief that small farms have higher per hectare productivity.

---

7. See, Desai (n.d.): 385-88. I have examined this phenomenon in the context of the wheat growers and have arrived at the same conclusion. See, Vyas (forthcoming).

Aggregate data for Gujarat do indicate that a proportionately larger area is under irrigation on small farms. According to the agricultural census, as against the overall percentage of 10.4 (i.e., the percentage of total cropped area irrigated), the area under irrigation in different categories of small farms varied from 14.2 per cent on the holding below 0.5 ha to 12.5 per cent on farms from 1-2 ha in size. However, there are two significant facts, the importance of which is not fully recognised. In the first place, in the state as a whole, a much small proportion of small farms (16-22%) have any irrigation facility as compared with large farms (above 40%). Secondly, in a number of regions in the state, the proportion of irrigated area to the total cultivated area is less on small farms. The Surat and Matar studies both report less than average area under irrigation on small farms. Taken together, these findings mean that only a few areas and that too only on a relatively small number of such farms is the area irrigated, in proportionate terms, above average.

Further, it ought to be remembered that in absolute terms, the irrigated area on small farms does not amount to much. Even if all the irrigated area were to be double cropped, 'land expanding' effect of this would be insignificant. On an average, for a five acre farm, it would not 'add' even an acre of land. In reality, the percentage of area sown more than once is much less than the area under irrigation, and small farms do not fare better than large or medium-sized farms in this context (Desai, n.d.: 87, Table 4.6).

Such a meagre and less productive land base has an important consequence. The small farmers' households have to place an increasing reliance on subsidiary occupations like dairying and agricultural labour. Relevant information on this aspect is available only from the Surat survey. During the period covered by the study, the dependence of the 'earners' and 'helpers' on cultivation remained more or less constant, whereas there was a marked change in subsidiary occupations of the family members of small holders. The dependence on craft as a secondary source of income was more or less eliminated, and that on dairy markedly increased (Desai, n.d.: Tables 3.17-3.20).

Finally, information from the regional studies clearly reveals that the investment on agricultural improvement in small farms is very meagre. Thus, by adding the four-year data from 1968-69 to 1970-71 of the Surat study, we find that per acre outlay on agricultural improvement during the given period was the lowest on small farms (₹25.63) and the highest on medium-sized farms (₹78.78). This not only suggests a low level of investment for agricultural improvement on small farms, but also augurs ill for the future prospect of improvement of the land base of similar conclusions. The authors of the Matar Survey had already warned:

> A smaller marketable surplus leading to lower cash incomes and smaller expenditure on such modern inputs as fertilisers smaller investible resources with relatively greater need for investment in traditional items have acted and are likely to act as obstacles to the progress of the small farmers. The inevitable result would be a widening of the income gap between the small and big farmers (Shah and Shah, 1974: 263-64).

The above details more or less complete the picture of immiseration of small farms during the last decade or so and also serve as a pointer to the shape of things to come if immediate steps are not taken.

III

By emphasising that in Gujarat, we have witnessed the phenomenon of immiseration rather than proletarianisation, are we only quibbling with words? I do not think so. The fact that an overwhelmingly large number of small farmers has been able to retain their land, and also the fact that the inadequate net output from their land do not allow them to make two ends meet and hence forces them to rely on agricultural labour and other supplementary occupations in a progressively large measure, suggest a different type of dynamics operating in the countryside than what is normally assumed. It also suggests the possible lines of action. However, it is not my intention at this stage to dilate on the latter; I shall try to explain the working of the forces which have resulted in the situation described above.

The explanation of these phenomena has to be sought in the functioning of the land, labour and capital markets in the context of the available technology. From all available evidence, the land market in the state is almost frozen. The only active element seems to be the large farmers selling off their land to the medium-sized and sometimes even the small farmers. In Western India, particularly in Gujarat, land reforms of the mid-1950s and the early 1960s enabled large number of landless tenants and small tenants to obtain ownership rights in land. It is true that all those who were entitled to get land did not receive it. It is also true that a section of the erstwhile tenants who received land were ejected from the land in the subsequent years. Yet there is enough evidence to prove that a sizeable redistribution of land did take place following the land reform legislation (Dantwala and Shah, 1971). Also, a greater convergence of ownership and management took place and tenancy as a category of relationship in land declined to a considerable extent.

The subsequent developments, particularly the emerging socio-economic milieu, made the ejectment of small farmers from land all the more difficult. The ceiling laws, however clumsily implemented, made it extremely risky for the large farmers to expand their holdings. The emergent group of the progressive medium-sized farmers found that given the high-productivity, high-cost technology, it was more profitable to invest on their existing holdings and strengthen their land base, e.g., by expanding irrigation facilities, rather than purchasing more land. These were the demand constraints on the land markets. On the supply side, the fact that the alternative for the small farmers was not migration to urban areas for being absorbed in the urban-industrial workforce, but in supplementing their incomes by auxiliary occupations like agricultural labour and dairying, considerably weakened the compulsion to sell off land. The process of proletariatisation was halted by these forces on the demand and supply sides. Yet the situation as it obtains today is far from ideal.

Now the main levers of exploitation are credit and marketing institutions. The seasonal nature of agricultural employment means a period of low economic activity, and the low returns on land result in low or non-existent reserves. Thus, during the off-season, the small and marginal farmers have to depend on consumption loans from bigger landlords, moneylenders or traders. The collateral provided and sought is either the crops raised on the small farmers' fields or some form of bonded labour to work on larger farms.

It argues well that the attention of policymakers has now shifted to the abolition of bonded labour as well as the usurious arrangements for credit. The legislative measures, however, cannot go far enough. Unless an alternative source of consumption loans is provided, all these efforts are bound to fail and the process of immiseration will continue unabated. Even alternative sources of consumption credit will only be able to provide some marginal, though important, relief. The basic problem—their weak economy—cannot be solved by consumption loans or any other palliative of this nature.

Hence the question which has to be squarely faced is: Do we want to create a viable small farm sector in our country or do we only want the process of consolidation of land into larger—or medium-sized if you like—holding to be made smooth and easy? Obviously, these alternatives have to be considered within a time frame. Suppose, we were to consider the problem in the perspective of a decade from now, what approach should we recommend?

If we rule out the alternative of big-push industrialisation or for that matter any large-scale off-farm employment programme which can absorb all the 'surplus' labour on land—an alternative in which once the numbers involved are given can hardly be considered feasible, the problem of small farms can be tackled by two distinct approaches These are:

- Facilitating the creation of an agrarian structure with large and medium-sized farms, and enabling small farmers to get employment on these farms on reasonable terms (in other words, to accept proletarianisation as a historical necessity and 'humanise' the process).
- Strengthening the land base of small farms by evolving suitable technology and organisational structures to support small farms and to facilitate related occupations on small farms.

As a good strategy and in the tradition of the social scientists in this country, the best thing for me would be to stop after posing this question. Yet I wish to seek your indulgence and to make brief comments on two implicit assumptions, which have to be made while supporting one or the other alternative. The first relates to the creation and mobilisation of surpluses and the second to the process by which the eventual shift from agricultural to non-agricultural sector can take place.

Once we rule out the possibility of big-push industrialisation, it becomes obvious that the agricultural sector will have to generate surpluses, not only for maintaining a certain level of productivity on land, but also for reinvesting a part of these to raise the production potential. At present, only a small proportion of the farms are in a position to do so. These are, by and large, bigger holdings. But a relevant question is: Can we step up the surpluses on this narrow base of large/medium-sized peasantry to a level that gainful employment can be provided to rest of the rural workforce either by way of direct employment on these surplus-generating farms or indirectly by the secondary round of activities generated by such surpluses. My hypothesis, and at this stage it is no more than that, is that the activity of surplus creation will have to be more broad based. In other words, bulk of the small farmers will have to be brought into the surplus-creating stream. Is it impossible?

Since we have not looked carefully for alternative institutional arrangements to provide credit and modern inputs to small farms or generate an appropriate technology for them—mainly because of our familiarity with the surplus-generating sector in Western agriculture —we tend to rule it out, more or less, by definition. If, however, one were to look into the agrarian structure in some of the South Asian countries, including large parts of Japan, Taiwan, Malaysia, Thailand and many parts of Ceylon, one is struck by the fact that a one hectare farm in these areas is a surplus-generating unit. Hence, creation of an economically viable small farm sector cannot be entirely ruled out.

Any programme to revitalise the small farm sector runs against our notion of the eventual diversification of the economy. It can be readily agreed that we should not support the small farm sector in a manner that it makes the eventual shift from agricultural to non-agricultural sector difficult or costly or both. Where one can have difference is the manner in which the envisaged shift from agriculture to non-agriculture sector may take place. A pattern that has emerged in some countries is the diversification of activities on the small farms—a thing which has been recorded in our state also—by the inclusion of dairying and wage-paid employment apart from cultivation. Is it not possible that at a certain stage, these subsidiary activities will become primary activities and a process of specialisation may start?

The idea of establishing a viable small farm sector includes actions on various fronts, particularly on the institutional, organisational and technological planes. It is not my intention to provide a blue-print for action, for the simple reason that I do not know enough. What makes me optimistic in regard to organisation of the small farm sector on a viable basis is the possibility of major restructuring of our institution, like of which we have already availed. For example, the very fact that we could institute land reforms, which aimed at fundamental alterations in property rights, should give confidence for instituting similar, far-reaching institutional changes in the field of credit and marketing. It ought to be recognised that to tamper with the ownership of land is a far more difficult decision, both because land is a naturally limited resource and the whole power structure in the countryside revolves round it. Yet the fact that it could be attempted in all seriousness suggests the capability of the system for instituting far-reaching changes. While the temptation to comply with known constructs is an understandable one, we would be failing in our duty as social scientists if we miss the unique features of Indian rural dynamics or shun exploring a new path to development merely because it has not been traversed before.

References

Bhat, M.L. (1960). *Economic Survey of Borsad Taluka (Gujarat State).* Vallabh Vidyanagar: Agro-Economic Research Centre, Sardar Patel University. Mimeographed.

Dantwala, M.L. and C.H. Shah (1971). *Evaluation of Land Reforms* (Vol. 1). Bombay: University of Bombay. pp.35-60.

Krishnamurthy, J. (1972). "Working Force in 1971 Census: Some Exercise in Provisional Results", *Economic and Political Weekly* VII(5), January 15.

Saini, G.R. (1971). "Holding Size, Productivity and Some Related Aspects of Indian Agriculture", *Economic and Political Weekly*, June 26.

Shah, Vimal and C.H. Shah (1974). *Resurvey of Matar Taluka.* Bombay: Vora & Co. p.11.

Shah, Vimal and G. Repetto (1975). *Further Analysis of Data from the Resurvey of Matar Taluka.* Boston: Harvard University Centre for Population Studies. pp.7-15. Mimeographed.

Vyas, V.S. (1968). "Economic Efficiency on Small Farms of Central Gujarat", *Seminar on Problems of Small Farmers, Bombay: Indian Society of Agricultural Economics.* pp.60-75.

————. (forthcoming). "High Yielding Varieties in Wheat: The First Phase", *Mimeograph.* Mexico: International Wheat and Maize Research Institute.

Appendix A-4.1

Workers Engaged in Agriculture Proper in 1961 and 1971 on Comparable Basis (Gujarat and All-India)
(1961 Adjusted as per 1971 Definitions)

(Figures in 000)

		Cultivators	*Agricultural Workers*	*Other Workers*	*Total Workers*	*Population*
Gujarat	Males 1961 adjusted	2,765 (64.39)	640 (14.90)	889 (20.71)	4,294 (100)	7,830
	1971	3,070 (59.04)	1,184 (22.77)	946 (18.19)	5,200 (100)	9,843
	Females 1961 adjusted	1,261 (64.89)	434 (22.35)	248 (12.76)	1,943 (100)	7,447
	1971	438 (38.79)	609 (53.94)	82 (7.27)	1,129 (100)	9,358
	Total 1961 adjusted	4,026 (64.55)	1.074 (17.22)	1,137 (18.23)	6,237 (100)	15,317
	1971	3,508 (55.43)	1,793 (28.33)	1,028 (16.24)	6,329 (100)	19,201
All India	Male 1961 adjusted	64,374 (61.64)	15,986 (15.31)	24,081 (23.05)	104,441 (100)	183,357
	1971	67,417 ((55.99)	30,359 (25.22)	22,632 (18.79)	120,408 (100)	225,219
	Female 1961 adjusted	27,248 (32.63)	10,205 (54.39)	7,866 (12.98)	45,319 (100)	176,643
	1971	9,127 (32.63)	15,211 (54.39)	3,629 (12.98)	27,967 (100)	213,637
	Total 1961 adjusted	91,622 (61.18)	26,191 (17,49)	31,947 (21.33)	149,760 (100)	360,000
	1971	76,544 (51.59)	45,570 (30.71)	26,261 (17.70)	148,375 (100)	438,856

Note : Figures in the parenthesis indicate percentages to total workers.

Source : Census of India 1971-Series I-Indian Miscellaneous Studies: Paper of 1974 "Report on Resurvey on Economic Questions - Some Results" – Registrar General's Office, New Delhi.

Appendix A-4.2

Number and Area under Different Size-Groups of Holidings in 1960-61 and 1971-72

(Figures in 000)

	1960-61			1970-71		
Size Class of Operational Holdings (acres)	*No of Operational Holdings*	*Area Operated*	*Average Area*	*No. of Operational Holdings*	*Area Operated*	*Average Area*
Small farm (up to 4.99)	5,580 (33.90)	13,860 (7.07)	2.48	11,188 (47.89)	28,373 (13.39)	2.54
Medium farm (5-24.99)	8,880 (53.95)	102,530 (52.30)	11.55	10,255 (43.89)	112,051 (52.88)	10.93
Large farm (25 and above)	2000 (12.15)	79670 (40.63)	39.84	1921 (8.22)	71,457 (33.73)	37.20
All Classes	16460 (100)	196,060 (100)	11.91	23,364 (100)	211,881 (100)	9.07

Note : Figures in parenthesis are percentages to total.

Source: NSS Round 16 and 26 (Central Sample).

Number and Area under Different Size-Groups of Holidings in 1960-61 and 1971-72

(Reference Base: 1964-65)

	Matar				Nadiad			
Size Class	*Gross from Above*	*Arrivals from Below*	*Gross Departure*	*Net Arrivals*	*Gross from Below*	*Arivals from Above*	*Gross Departure*	*Net Arrivals*
Small	14	116	9	121	9	52	9	52
Medium	13	68	14	67	3	44	9	38
Big	1	32	13	20	2	13	3	12
Large	0	8	1	7	0	1	2	–1

Source: Dantwala and Shah (1971: 87).

Appendix A-4.3

Size-wise Cropping Pattern, Gujarat (1970-71)

(Areas in hectares

Size Class (in ha)	Gross Cropped Area	Percentage of Gross Cropped Area Allotted to the Following Food Crops				
		Rice	Jawar	Bajri	Wheat	Maize
Below 05	84.69	25.8	6.0	25.2	4.2	4.6
0.5-1.0	2,33,522	15.2	7.8	26.4	4.3	4.9
1.0-2.0	7,12,652	10.8	8.9	24.2	4.5	5.4
2.0-3.0	8,32,361	10.8	9.3	22.3	4.8	5.3
3.0-4.0	8,19,215	7.8	9.6	1.3	5.0	4.6
4.0-5.0	8,09,388	6.7	10.1	20.9	5.1	3.8
5.0-10.0	30,41,417	4.5	10.5	20.6	5.6	2.3
10.0-20.0	27,07,697	2.0	12.4	22.4	6.2	0.8
Over 20.0	8,54,490	1.4	144.3	25.6	6.2	0.7

Size Class (in ha)	Percentage of Area under All Food Crops	Percentage of Gross Cropped Area Allotted to			Percentage of Area under All Non-Food Crops
		Groundnut	Cotton	Tobacco	
Below 0.5	79.0	3.2	8.6	2.0	21.0
0.5-10	72.4	6.1	12.5	2.2	27.6
1.0-2.0	67.2	9.4	14.7	1.9	32.8
2.0-3.0	53.3	12.3	15.5	1.5	36.2
3.0-4.0	60.8	15.0	16.0	1.3	39.2
4.0-5.0	58.5	17.1	16.4	1.0	41.5
5.0-10.0	53.3	21.6	17.6	0.5	46.7
10.0-20.0	51.0	22.6	19.2	0.1	49.0
Over 20.0	55.3	14.2	20.1	0.1	44.7

Source: Agricultural Census, 1970-71.

5

Marginalised Sections of Indian Agriculture

*The Forgotten Millions**

Introduction

There is widespread concern in the country about the stagnation in agricultural production. This, together with the falling prices of agricultural produce and the rising prices of agricultural inputs, has seriously affected the economy of a large number of farmers. The well-being of millions of families dependent on agriculture for their livelihood is jeopardised. The spate of suicides by agricultural producers in different parts of the country is a stark manifestation of these developments. A large number of people in the farm sector are witnessing serious erosion in their incomes and welfare. All this is happening at a time when the GDP (gross domestic product) growth in the country has been increasing at the rate of 6-7 per cent during the last few years, with a prospect of further acceleration in this trend. This paper addresses the plight of the marginal sections of the peasantry, the reasons for decline in their incomes and the possible approaches to strengthen their income-earning capacity. It argues that the constituents of a large section of Indian agriculture, because of their weak asset base, have limitations in responding to economic stimuli on their own and therefore, need special attention.

Generally, two approaches are followed in our country to identify marginalised sections of the population. One takes the geographical route, i.e., identifying 'backward areas' in terms of natural hazards, inaccessibility, lack of infrastructure, etc., and categorises the producers in such areas as the disadvantaged sections. Special programmes to

* Presidential address delivered at the 48th Annual Coference of Indian Society of Labour Economics organised by Bharathidasan University, Trichurapalli, 5 January 2007.

develop the backward districts are based on this assumption. The Tenth Plan identified 150 districts as 'backward districts' and provided special assistance to the districts to develop infrastructure under the Rashtriya Sam Vikas Yojana (RSVY). The other approach is basically a sociological approach, and it identifies SCs (scheduled castes), STs (scheduled tribes), minorities and OBCs (other backward classes) as the marginalised sections. Several programmes and schemes have been launched to redress the inequity suffered by these groups. Both these approaches have limitations in identifying sections of the population who cannot respond to the stimuli provided by development. I would submit that the asset base of the household, rather than its location or social status, is the major determinant of its capacity to participate in the development process. In the rural sector of our country, it is access to land that, in my view, should determine whether or not a section should be identified as belonging to the marginalised sector.

For the purpose of our discussion, I shall treat the marginal farmers, i.e., those cultivating land below 1 ha, as the marginalised sections of the peasantry. These, along with landless labourers and rural artisans, account for the bulk of the disadvantaged sections in rural society. I shall concentrate on the first of these three groups, partly because both scholars as well as policymakers give very little attention to this group. The scholars club them with agricultural labourers, as labour contributes a substantial part of their income. Policymakers concerned with agricultural production and its contribution to GDP do not treat them as a significant section of producers and tend to write them off as they are not supposed to contribute to agricultural growth to any remarkable measure. Two important objections can be raised to considering land as the proxy for the asset base of the rural household. In the first place, land may be one of the assets of a household. There may be other avenues of income, which a farmer may be able to avail himself of, e.g., wage labour, animal husbandry, etc. However, here we are concerned with the income-earning capacity of the households, which consider agricultural income as the principal source of their income and land as their main asset. Besides, their access to other assets is also seriously conditioned by access to land.

Secondly, it has been suggested, and rightly so, that land cannot be considered as being of uniform quality. A hectare of land in an arid and infertile area cannot be equated to a hectare of land in irrigated, fertile tracts. Yet, even in the fertile regions, people at the bottom of the ladder are likely to have limited wherewithal. Of course, the plight of the marginal farmers will be worse in the dry, unfertile regions. I shall, therefore, concentrate on farmers operating landholdings of 1 ha or less. It may be noted that SC and ST households, to the extent they are cultivators, are largely marginal farmers. Thus, in the case of a large number of rural households, social deprivation and low asset base converge.

In the first two sections, I shall identify the extent and growth of marginal farmers in the country as a whole, as well as in different states, and spell out the factors which have led to a remarkable increase in their number and the area cultivated by them. In the next section, I shall introduce the current status of their economy with the help of some indicators. The fourth section reviews the policies and programmes, which may impinge on their economy and the options available to them for improving their economic status. The last section concludes the discussion.

Agrarian Structure in India

Two prominent features of the Indian economy have hardly changed over the last few decades. These are: (i) an overwhelming proportion of the Indian population lives in the rural areas and (ii) there is no significant diversification of the rural economy. According to the 2001 Census, 72.2 per cent of the population of the country lives in the rural areas. In 1951, this proportion was 82.7 per cent. Thus, over the period of five decades, the share of rural population in the total population was declining at the rate of nearly 2 per cent per decade. Figures for different states vary. However, the latest (2001) Population Census has revealed that out of 17 major states of the country, only five (Tamil Nadu, Maharashtra, Gujarat, Karnataka and Punjab) have recorded more than one-third of their population as 'urban' mainly because of the rapid growth of population in their capital cities. Over the last few decades, for the country as a whole and for a large majority of the states, the composition of population, in terms of 'rural' and 'urban' has not changed in any remarkable way. An equally significant feature is the overwhelming dependence on agriculture for livelihood in the rural areas. According to the 2001 Census, out of the total number of rural workers in the country, 73.3 per cent were employed in agriculture. In all major states, from over half to over three-fourth of the rural workforce were employed in agriculture, the only exception being Kerala (28.7%). However, the composition of the agricultural workforce in terms of cultivators and agricultural workers is changing, so is the size distribution of agricultural holdings. This suggests the need for a closer look at the agrarian structure.

Untill 1991, the proportion of agricultural workers, in the total agricultural workforce (cultivators + agricultural workers), was increasing only at a slow pace. The picture has changed since then as the proportion of agricultural workers has increased significantly, along with the rise in marginal farmers. More and more marginal farmers with small plots of land are opting for agricultural labour as their main occupation. This is reflected in the fact that more than half of the agricultural labour households possessed some land. (According to the 60th Round of the National Sample Survey [NSS], 56% of the agricultural labour households owned land between 0.4 and 1 ha). The increase in the agricultural workforce has mainly been due to the faster growth of marginal holdings, which could not provide adequate gainful employment to their operators. This process has accelerated in recent years. More and more agricultural households are entering the category of marginal farmers. (Table 5.1 gives the number of marginal farmers and the area held by them.) It is seen that during the course of the quarter century, from 1970-71 to 1995-96, the number of marginal holdings as a proportion of the total holdings has increased from about half (50.62%) to over 60 per cent (61.58%), while the area cultivated in these holdings has increased from 8.97 per cent to 17.21 per cent of the total cultivated area. Major changes can be summarised as follows:

- The proportion of agricultural workers in the agricultural workforce has increased. However, the proportion of landless labourers in the total number of agricultural workers has not increased.

- The landholding structure in India is sliding downwards, with progressively greater concentration in the marginal holdings group.
- Not only is the number of marginal holdings increasing, but the area cultivated in such holdings is alsoexpanding. The proportion of the area under medium and semi-medium holdings accounts for nearly half of the agricultural area, and has remained more or less constant.

Table 5.1

Number and Area under Marginal Holdings from 1970-71 to 1995-96

Year	*Number ('000)*			*Area ('000 ha)*		
	All Groups	*Number of Marginal Holdings*	*Percentage of Marginal Holdings*	*All Groups*	*Area Operated by Marginal Holdings*	*Percentage of Area of Marginal Holdings*
1970-71	70490	35680	50.62	162120	14550	8.97
1976-77	81570	44520	54.58	163340	17510	10.72
1980-81	88880	50120	56.39	163800	19730	12.05
1985-86	97160	56150	57.79	164560	22040	13.39
1990-91	105290	62110	58.99	165600	24620	14.87
1995-96	115580	71179	61.58	163357	28121	17.21

Source: Centre for Monitoring Indian Economy (CMIE), Agriculture, March 2006.

- There has been a significant decline in the number of large holdings as well as the area cultivated in them.
- The area reported under tenancy is relatively small—around 8 per cent—even though there is a large amount of concealed tenancy.
- All size groups of landholdings participate as both lessors as well as lessees.

Among these salient features of the agrarian structure, the most noteworthy is the increase in the number and the area under marginal holdings. In 1995-96, the latest year for which agricultural Census data are available for the country as a whole and for individual states in the required detail, 71.2 million of the cultivated holdings were in the size group of 1 ha or less. About 28.1 million ha of land was cultivated by this size group of farmers. As mentioned earlier, over a period of time, the number as well as the area under cultivation in this size-group of holdings has been escalating. In 1970-71, these holdings accounted for 51 per cent of the total cultivated holdings. A decade later, the proportion rose to 56 per cent. The Census of 1995-96 suggests that their share in the total holdings has reached 62 per cent. Over 71 million cultivators in the country were operating holdings of 1 ha or less. If the past trends were to continue, by 2005-06, nearly 14 million holdings would have been added to this category, bringing the total to 85 million holdings. It is generally recognised that a large majority of cultivators in our country are marginal farmers. However, what is noteworthy is the fact that a progressively increasing share of cultivated land is farmed by this group. In 1970-71, nearly 9 per cent of the land was cultivated in holdings of 1 ha or less. A decade later, the proportion of land cultivated in marginal holdings was 12 per cent of the cultivated area. By 1995-96, their share in the total cultivated land rose to 17 per cent. If the same trends had continued, by now, the marginal farmers would have been cultivating nearly 20 per cent of our land. Already, by 1995-96, one-third or more of the cultivated area in five states—Kerala (53%), West Bengal (WB) (43%), Jammu & Kashmir (J&K) (40%), Bihar (36%) and Uttar Pradesh (UP) (34%)—was in marginal holdings and one more state, Tamil Nadu (TN), was close to joining their ranks (see Table 5.2). Thus, the marginal farmers not only constitute an overwhelming majority of the cultivators, but are becoming increasingly important as agricultural producers too.

Nearly half (48%) of the total number of marginal farmers are located in three states: UP (23%), Bihar (16%) and Andhra Pradesh (AP) (9%). These three states, together with TN (8%) and Kerala (8%), account for nearly two-third of the marginal farmers in the country. On the other land, each of the following states, Punjab, Haryana, Himachal Pradesh (HP), Gujarat and J&K have less than 1 per cent of the country's marginal farmers. In terms of area also, more or less the same ranking prevails. The largest area under marginal holdings is in UP (including 22.3% of the country's total area under marginal holdings), followed by Bihar (13.8%) and AP (10.3%). Punjab and

Table 5.2

Number and Area under Marginal Holdings in Different States in 1985-86 and 1995-96

State	Number ('000)				Area ('000 ha)			
	1985-86	% to Total Operational Holdings	1995-96	% to total Operational Holdings	1985-86	% to Total Operational Holdings	1995-96	% to Total Operational Holdings
AP	4461	54.20	6300	59.42	2053	14.50	2904	20.20
Assam	1451	59.98	1669	62.21	600	18.98	621	19.79
Bihar	8976	76.65	11344	80.14	3303	30.31	3871	36.24
Gujarat	801	25.47	1034	27.35	416	4.18	562	5.67
Haryana	502	37.27	815	47.16	229	6.17	404	10.99
Himachal Pradesh	463	61.49	556	64.43	201	20.51	230	23.00
J&K	875	73.84	1041	77.92	335	32.68	402	39.68
Karnataka	1792	36.43	2610	41.95	866	7.29	1248	10.31
Kerala	3993	90.59	5918	93.95	810	45.84	912	53.27
Madhya Pradesh	2733	35.95	3878	40.38	1214	5.48	1795	8.20
Maharashtra	2488	30.71	4266	40.05	1232	5.77	2087	10.50
Odisha	1868	52.09	2145	54.08	919	17.47	1064	20.68
Punjab	256	23.53	204	18.66	139	3.39	122	2.94
Rajasthan	1358	28.63	1611	30.03	641	3.11	780	3.67
Tamil Nadu	5498	71.34	5951	74.28	2018	25.89	2210	30.26
UP	13782	72.59	16237	75.42	4993	28.29	6266	33.74
West Bengal	4343	70.85	5003	76.42	1821	32.27	2399	42.93
All India	56147	57.79	71179	61.58	22042	13.39	28121	17.21

Note: Available data suggest that there is larger area recorded as 'owned' than the area reported as 'operated.' Presumably, palpably small holdings are leased out or left uncultivated.

Source: Agricultural Statistics at a Glance, Ministry of Agriculture, Government of India, New Delhi.

HP have less than 1 per cent of the country's cultivated area in this category. A major concentration of the marginal farmers, in terms of numbers as well as area, is in the three states of UP, Bihar and AP.

Significant changes have taken place in recent years in the agrarian structure in different states of the country. Thus, during the decade of 1985-86 to 1995-96, the number of marginal farmers in the total number of cultivators rose in the states of Gujarat, Maharashtra, MP, Odisha and Karnataka. It may be noted that even a decade ago, these were not states with high shares of marginal holdings (i.e., greater than average for the country as a whole). They seem to be 'progressing' to attain that rank. On the other hand, there is a proportionate decline in the share of marginal holdings in the total holdings in a few states, most notably in Kerala and Punjab, but also in WB, UP and TN; while in Haryana, the share of marginal farmers in the total number has remained more or less stable. A similar picture is obtained in the share of area in the total cultivated area of the states. The area under marginal holdings has declined in Punjab, WB and Kerala, but has increased in Maharashtra, Gujarat and MP. If the gross value of agriculture per hectare of cultivated land is taken as an indicator of commercialisation, with the exception of UP, then all the states, where there had been a proportionate decline in the share of marginal holdings, had high value of agricultural produce per hectare, as compared to the average value in the country as a whole.

Broadly, the following picture emerges from the above-mentioned facts:

- For the country as a whole, marginal farmers constitute the largest segment of agricultural holdings, with the major concentration in UP, Bihar and AP.
- Practically in all states of the country, marginal holdings accounted for an overwhelming majority of the total holdings in each state. The share of land cultivated under these holdings in a number of states was one-third, or more, of the total cultivated area of the respective state.
- In most of the states, and in the country as a whole, the number of marginal cultivators and the area cultivated by them are increasing.

- Only in a limited number of states, has there been a fall in the number of marginal farmers as well as in the area cultivated by them. These are, with a few exceptions, the states with high value of gross produce per hectare.

It will be instructive to see the dynamics and logic of these changes. This task is addressed in the following section.

Factors Affecting Changes in the Agrarian Structure

Changes in agrarian structure, which were observed in the previous section, are based on periodic censuses and surveys. At best, they give a comparative picture at different points of time. They do not reveal the processes that account for such changes, nor do they indicate inter-group or intra-group dynamics, which result in the observed changes. Only panel data over large parts of the country can yield such information. In the absence of regularly monitored intra-group data, we have to make a qualitative assessment by analysing the likely impact of some of the determining factors on structural changes in landholdings and access to land by different groups. These factors can be broadly categorised as: (i) market transactions, (ii) legislative measures, and (iii) demographic factors.

Land Market

In traditional societies, transactions in land are not very common because until a dire need arises, a peasant does not like to sell his land. However, in the pre-Independence era, large chunks of land had passed over from the peasants to moneylenders mainly for settling debts, or to landlords because of the peasants' failure to pay rent, especially during the drought years. These were not purely market-induced transactions; an element of coercion was always present. During the post-Independence period, the process of expropriation seems to have slowed down. Provisions of various legislations have also contributed to restrictions on land transfers. For example, a ST landowner cannot sell his/her land to a non-ST person.

Opportunities for intensification of farming, especially in the irrigated area, lured cultivators with cash surpluses to invest in the existing holdings, rather than expand their holdings. On the other hand, tenancy legislation ('land to the tiller'), enacted in a number of states, made it possible for the landless or marginal tenants to purchase the land, which they had been cultivating on lease. Admittedly, this was not a universal phenomenon. But, in the areas where absentee landlords were lessors, it was not an uncommon feature. This tendency was more prominent wherein the credit institutions, i.e., land development banks, advanced credit to tenants for purchase of land, e.g., in parts of the former Bombay and Saurashtra states. Available evidence suggests that in the initial years of land reforms in the country, the land market tended to work in favour of the small and marginal landowners, rather than against them (Dantwala and Shah, 1971).

The situation has changed to a certain extent, with large chunks of land being acquired by the state, or by private entrepreneurs, with the active assistance of the state, for non-farm activities. The net cultivated area in the country has gone down in recent years mainly because of such acquisitions. However, 'purchases' of land, e.g., for creating housing colonies or SEZs (special economic zones), have not specifically targeted marginal holdings. The bias is towards acquiring land where it is available in bigger chunks. At the same time, there is some indication of an active land market, at least a lease market, in the states where commercialisation of agriculture has taken greater strides, e.g., in Punjab, as reflected in the diminishing number of marginal holdings.

Land Reforms

Legislation pertaining to land reforms played a much more important role in influencing the ownership pattern. Market-related factors at best supplemented the impact of land legislation. The direct implication of the ceiling legislation in sequestering the land of large owners and its distribution to small and marginal farmers, as is well known, was not significant, except in J&K and WB. But the indirect pressure exerted by the legislation was very significant. In spite of fictitious transfers and other subterfuges devised by the large landowners, enactment of land ceiling legislation led to disposal of land by those owning large holdings, particularly the absentee landlords. As the tenancy legislation gave the right of purchase of land to the tenants, the process of breaking up of the above ceiling holdings was further accentuated. In any event, the ceiling legislation made it more risky to enlarge holdings beyond the stipulated area and, to that extent, curbed the tendency to further enlarge the holdings by dispossessing small owners and acquiring their land. It is reasonable to infer that the small farmers could retain their holdings against machinations of the large farmers and they, as well as the landless labourers, were the main beneficiaries once larger landowners decided to dispose of part of their land, to be on the right side of the law. Again, the process did not unfold in a neat fashion. There were large numbers of ejections of small tenants as there were numerous cases of acquisition of land by small farmers. However, in large parts of the country, small landowners and landless tenants were the gainers due to land reform legislation.

Demographic Pressure

While increase in the area under the marginal and smallholding group could be largely explained by the legislative measures supplemented by market processes, their rising number is basically due to an increase in population in those households and lack of alternative employment opportunities in the countryside. An expansion of the household or, more commonly, death of the household head leads to division of the holding among the legal heirs. Unfortunately, there are no systematic studies of household dynamics in the rural areas of our country to enable us to arrive at a precise measure of sub-division of holdings due to demographic factors over a period of time. However, it is reasonable to assume that the combined effect of the two factors, population growth and lack of non-farm employment opportunities, largely explains the rise in the number of small and marginal holdings. There could also be a possibility of 'ladder', i.e., landless labourers, or more likely landless tenants acquiring small plots of land. In the circumstances discussed above, this possibility cannot be ruled out. Similarly, a decline in the number of large and big holding groups and the area under them could be due to the division of households leading to sub-divisions of the holdings and their sliding down to the lower holding group. At the same time, reduction in the number of households in these holding groups, due to their decision to opt for non-farm activities, could also be one of the reasons for the diminishing numbers in this holding group. A confluence of the factors described above has resulted in small-farm-dominated agriculture in our country. This tendency is likely to continue. Given the present social and political milieu, it may be possible to stop the erosion of the holdings of small farmers, but it will not be possible to stop the division of large holdings. Their further expansion to any meaningful extent is out of question, the noise about corporatisation of agriculture or removal of ceiling notwithstanding. Agriculture, dominated by small farms, will be a reality in India for quite some time to come.

Economy of the Marginal Farmers

Obviously, we cannot ignore the well-being of more than 80 million farmers cultivating holdings below 1 ha. Before we discuss the ameliorating measures, it will be useful to understand the current status of their economy. Farmers belonging to this group sustain themselves mainly on what they can produce from their land, along with two other important activities, *viz.*, agricultural labour and animal husbandry. As far as their land resources are concerned, at the aggregate level, the area per holding has not changed over the last decade. In fact, there has been a marginal increase from 0.39 to 0.4 ha over the decade. These figures mask the group changes. However, there are some indications to suggest that there is a floor below which cultivation is generally not practised. Therefore, the quality of land that they operate, the crops they produce and the productivity of their resources are important determinants of the income they earn.

As far as quality of land is concerned, two different scenarios can be depicted. It can be presumed that if the marginalisation of agricultural holdings arises due to distribution and partitioning of the smallholdings, each successor will like to have land of comparable quality as his share. On the other hand, if lands of the small farmers are bought or sequestered by the bigger landowners and moneylenders, the land of better quality will have to be surrendered. I am inclined to assume that, generally, it is the former process, i.e., partitioning of the smallholdings due to demographic pressure, that is at work. However, in view of the fact that rapid deterioration of the land surface prevails all over the country, the poor farmers have their share of degraded land.

If we take irrigation as an indicator of more productive land, small and marginal farmers seem to be in an advantageous position. At the aggregate level, the small farmers have a larger proportion of area under irrigation, as a result of which they have a higher cropping intensity. However, they have to rely more on flow irrigation, largely from a public irrigation system. With the deceleration in expansion of flow irrigation and the deteriorating quality, the advantage, which this group enjoyed with regard to assured water supply, is fast disappearing. All the available evidence, which is mainly based on a decade-old agricultural census, clearly suggests that low-value cereals and other food crops dominate the cropping pattern on these holdings. The basic logic behind growing low-value food crops rests on the need for self-provisioning. With highly imperfect private markets for foodgrains in the rural areas, and low and inefficient penetration of the PDS (public distribution system) into these areas, this approach to crop planning is fully justifiable. There is another implication of the foodgrain-dominated cropping pattern of the marginal farmers. By 1990, nearly 19 per cent of the foodgrains were produced on marginal holdings. If the past trends continue, the share of these holdings in foodgrain production is likely to be more than 25 per cent by 2010. The productivity of crops on these holdings will have serious implications for the foodgrains economy of the country.

An aspect of the small-farm-dominated structure, which has not received as much attention as warranted, is its impact on inter-sectoral relationships. It appears that the impact of agricultural growth on poverty reduction has been weakening over a period of time. The changing agrarian pattern, with the ever-increasing weight of small and marginal farmers, provides some explanation for this phenomenon. With an increase in self-provisioning by this category of farmers, more of the marketable surplus is coming from larger holdings. In the consumption pattern of those (surplus-generating) households, goods and services from the organised urban sector dominate. As a result, the impact of agricultural growth on rural poverty is muted.

Discussions on the size–productivity relationship in Indian agriculture, which attracted a lot of attention in 1970s and 1980s, generally concluded that the yield per hectare for crops grown on the marginal and smallholdings was higher, though there were some dissenting voices even at that time. With the rising share of 'purchased' inputs in farming, the perceived advantages in terms of yield per hectare on the smallholdings (i.e., more intensive use of 'owned' resources) weakened considerably. In any event, changes in the dietary pattern, favouring a larger share of expenditure on non-foodgrain items will keep their income, real or imputed, highly subdued. The conclusion is inescapable that if the present trends continue, the marginal farmers will face the prospects of cultivating land of inferior quality, and raising foodgrains and other low-value crops. Even if the yields of these crops on the marginal holdings can be raised, it is doubtful whether their economic status can be improved substantially (Ali *et al.*, 1981).

Agricultural labour is the other important and, for many households in this category, the main source of income. Earnings from agricultural labour depend on the number of days of employment, and wages. Available studies suggest that the period of employment is shrinking, because of curtailment of the net cultivated area, the fast pace of mechanisation (e.g., in Punjab and Haryana) or transition to less labour-intensive cropping patterns (as in Kerala). The rising number of agricultural labourers, coupled with fuller employment of family labour, especially of women labourers in the family, has increased the labour pool. In sum, the elasticity of employment, with respect to output growth in agriculture, is approaching the near zero level. As Bhalla (2005) has remarked, "Agriculture has virtually ceased to employ more labour." Contraction of employment opportunities has adversely affected the income-earning prospects of marginal farmers.

The trends in agricultural wages suggest an increase in the real wages of agricultural labour in 1990s, but the rate of growth has decelerated as compared to that prevalent in 1980s. The increase in real wages was uneven, with the more progressive regions registering higher wages. (This may be a reason why the growth of marginal holdings in the prosperous regions is slower.) Female labour did not benefit to the extent that male labour did. With an increase in the proportion of casual labour, uncertainty with regard to wage earnings increased (Srivastava and Singh, 2006). In any event, marginal farmers 'tied' to their small pieces of land could not avail themselves of the benefits of peak season rise in wages. For this section of cultivators, the total wage earnings seem to have declined and uncertainty seems to have escalated.

The third major source of income for this group is animal husbandry and poultry. Emphasis on livestock (and poultry) is warranted for agricultural diversification so as to ensure higher income and employment as well as a strategy for risk mitigation. As in the case of the landholding structure, important changes are taking place in the animal husbandry sector also. Among these changes, the more important ones (as revealed in the NSS 59th Round) are listed as follows:

- A rise in the number of cattle, buffaloes and poultry slowed down in the 1990s, as compared to the preceding decade.
- Among bovines, the number of buffaloes is increasing rapidly, while the number of milch cattle is declining.
- There is a positive relationship between in-milk bovine stock and operational holdings; larger holdings can maintain larger bovine stock.
- There is a marked fall in the number of working cattle, i.e., bullocks, because of the diminishing importance of bullock power in crop cultivation and other allied activities.
- A positive feature is the spread of organised marketing in dairy products, especially in the cooperative sector.

The marginal holdings also experienced the impact of these changes in the livestock economy. They could retain their share of in-milk bovine stock; in fact, they increased it to some extent. But their share in buffaloes, which are emerging as the main dairy animals in the country, has declined. Their share in the bovine stock, in sheep and goats (more so in the latter), has slightly increased, along with their share in poultry stock. Overall, the changing composition of the livestock and poultry stocks on marginal holdings has placed them in a disadvantageous position, especially in the more remunerative dairy sector.

Another important source of income for workers in the marginal holding group could be wage labour in non-farm occupations. In general, wages in the non-farm sector are higher as compared to farm wages for the country as a whole, as well as in most of the states. However, available information suggests that during the post-reform period, i.e., in 1990s, the wages of causal workers in the non-farm sector registered a slower rate of growth as compared to the previous decade. The real problem, as far as the non-farm sector is concerned, is the slow growth in employment opportunities. As was mentioned earlier, only a slow process of diversification of the rural economy was observed during the last quarter century or more. The causes as well as the consequences of slow growth in the rural non-farm sector have been carefully analysed by several scholars.

The general conclusions emerging from these studies are as follows:

- Sluggish growth in employment in the non-farm sector, which seems to have further slowed down in 1990s.
- Among the non-farm activities, relatively higher growth in the tertiary sector, e.g., construction, trade, transport and communication.
- Fast casualisation of the workforce in these sectors in the rural areas.

It is reasonable to assume that employment opportunities for marginal farmers in the non-farm sector have not increased, except, may be, in the construction sector, and the nature of employment is becoming progressively ad hoc and intermittent. The obvious conclusion thus is that the plight of a large, in fact the largest, section of the rural population, the marginal farmers, has worsened over a period of time. The rural economy cannot be rejuvenated unless special attention is given to this section of the rural population.

Towards New Agriculture

It is clear from the above discussion that Indian agriculture is essentially small farm agriculture, and this feature is likely to become more prominent in the coming years. The possibility of a large 'exodus' from agriculture to the non-agricultural sectors in the near future can be ruled out. Agricultural strategy should treat this as the starting point for any reform in, or rejuvenation of, the agricultural sector. The moot question, therefore, is what can be done to improve the living conditions of a vast section of the rural population subsisting on small and marginal holdings and to bring them into the mainstream of development. In view of the emerging structure of Indian agriculture, the following three-pronged strategy can be adopted to strengthen the economy of a vast majority of farmers, and simultaneously, to make Indian agriculture a dynamic sector:

- increasing the asset base of the small and marginal farmers;
- improving productivity, especially value addition, on these farms; and
- increasing the scope for non-farm employment.

It needs to be emphasised at the outset that these are not alternative strategies, and in most situations, they can be made complementary to each other. Also, these strategies will succeed to the extent that: (i) supportive institutions for research, extension, marketing and credit assist the emerging structure, (ii) farmers organise themselves to avail of better bargaining positions, and (iii) effective measures are taken to mitigate risks in production and marketing.

Access to Land

An asset of the marginal farmers, which distinguishes them from other marginalised sections of the rural population, is their land. Access to land also determines access to other resources. The possibilities of expanding the land base of marginal farmers should be explored. In the past also, ceiling legislations were enacted in different states with the objective of sequestering land from large holdings and distributing the same to landless labourers or marginal farmers. By all accounts, with the exception of one or two states, the effort was a failure. The area declared surplus was barely 7 million acres (about 2.8 million hectares), of which 6.5 million acres was taken possession of and 5.4 million acres was distributed among 5.6 million households, with each of them receiving, on an average, less than an acre of land.

A new phase of market-friendly land reforms, as against the confiscatory type of land reforms—the days for which are over—is necessary. This, of course, does not preclude effective implementation of the existing laws. But, one should not have high hopes of getting additional land for redistribution in any substantial measure through this route. The next phase of land reforms should be based on the following two major initiatives:

- Small farmers should be encouraged, and enabled, to expand their holdings by purchasing or by leasing-in land.
- Large farmers should be encouraged to sell or lease out land and be offered opportunities to start non-farm rural enterprises.

As described above, the agrarian structure in our country is dominated by marginal holdings (i.e., holdings with less than 1 ha of cultivated land). Although with the declining importance of land in agriculture, the size of the holding is not the decisive criterion for remunerative farming, it can be safely assumed that barring some exceptional circumstances, 'the handkerchief holdings,' say of less than an acre, will no longer be viable. The objective should be to create as many 'viable' small farms as possible. It is erroneous to conclude from the above that estate farming is a better alternative. There is enough evidence to suggest that large holdings do not have any intrinsic advantage in crop production (Sen and Himanshu, 2004). We should aim at an agrarian structure characterised by small- and medium-sized holdings and enable them to carry out high-value, surplus-generating agriculture. A major step forward in that direction will be to permit farmers with very smallholdings to lease out their land to other marginal and small farmers on a long-term basis, without losing their ownership rights. In other words, in case of a number of marginal farmers, a ' ladder' can be put in place, permitting them to reach the higher category of landholdings. This will not be workable unless those who are leasing out their land retain their ownership right, and enough opportunities for non-farm employment are made available to them. For the latter to happen, large farmers should be encouraged to vacate (lease out) the land in favour of small farmers and specialise in post-harvest operations, trade, agroprocessing and other rural industries. This group has resources, access to institutional support and the capacity to bear risk, all of which are important for starting an enterprise.

These initiatives will be in accordance with what is actually happening at the ground level. At the two ends of the spectrum, i.e., among the farmers with miniscule holdings and those with large holdings, agriculture is not the main source of income. Of course, the sources of non-agricultural income differ in the two cases. The sources are wage income and income from livestock in the former case, and interest, profits and rent in the latter. The present arrangements of leasing out of land by the marginal as well as the large farmers are most often illegal and lead to sub-optimal results as the premium for the risk entailed in such arrangements is added on. In the past, i.e., during the initial phase of land reforms in our country, rural co-operative credit societies, especially the Land Development Banks (LDBs), assisted small farmers and tenants to buy land and enabled tenant farmers to secure proprietorship rights. Such schemes exist even today, but they hardly figure in the portfolio of rural financial institutions. In order to make this a viable strategy, the state will have to take various measures. These are discussed below.

(a) Unfreezing of the Lease Market

The objective of this measure is to enable small farms to increase their operational area. In order to ensure that it is not used to defeat the purpose of ceiling on agricultural holdings, it may be stipulated that the operational holdings with leased-in land should be within the ceiling limits. Further, the following three pre-conditions are necessary to achieve the objective of a 'free lease markets':

- proper record of rights;
- clear enunciation of rights and obligations of the landowner and the tenant;

- an effective machinery for monitoring and adjudication, at the ground level.

(b) Creation of an Active Land Market to Enable Small Farmers to Enlarge Their Holdings

On their own, small farmers will find it difficult to negotiate land purchase deals. Some agency of the state may thus purchase land at the market price from large farmers and sell it to the small farmers. The state is already playing this role when it comes to making land available for industry and infrastructure. In fact, many state agencies are creating 'land banks' to attract industries to their respective states. Why can the same not be done for marginal farmers in agriculture?

(c) Offering Financial Support to Small Farmers to Expand Their Holdings

Credit agencies should be encouraged to advance credit to small farmers for the purchase of land. This has been done in the past and is being done even today in some selected regions. Provisions for financing land purchases by the LDBs and re-financing of these advances by National Bank for Agriculture and Rural Development (NABARD) already exist. These have to be made more effective.

(d) Improving the Value of Agricultural Produce on the Small Farms

It was suggested earlier that value of the produce of the marginal farmers is low mainly because of the low-value crops and the low productivity on these holdings. Improving productivity on these farm holdings is an obvious component of the strategy for enhancing the income of small cultivators. At the same time, it should be recognised that in the case of minuscule holdings included in the marginal holding group, even a sizable increase in productivity, i.e., the yield per hectare, will not be able to lift them above the poverty line. There is a need to diversify their economy. Shifting from low-value to high-value crops is one of the forms of diversification of the farm economy. The other type of diversification calls for the use of resources in diverse but complementary activities (Vyas, 1996).

The introduction of high-value crops on these holdings is not easy because of the overarching compulsion of self-provisioning, coupled with high capital requirement and high risks entailed in raising such crops. A series of measures have to be taken to enable marginal farmers to shift from low-value subsistence crops to high-value commercial crops. Most important among these are measures for risk mitigation and adequate marketing arrangements.

Without first introducing proper and effective instruments of risk mitigation, asking the bulk of the farmers to go in for high input-intensive, highly riskprone, high-value crops is to compound their difficulties. In such circumstances, the better alternative will be to propagate mixed farming with emphasis on self-provisioning and 'commercial crops', or agriculture-related enterprises such as dairying is playing a supplementary role. This is the model which majority of the farmers in risk-prone areas are adopting on their own. The propagation of high-value agriculture in the Indian agricultural setting is predicated on the access to reliable instruments of crop and income insurance. The existing instruments, such as agricultural crop insurance to mitigate weather-induced risks, and MSP (minimum support prices) for the staple crops, are not functioning properly. These devices have obvious defects and therefore, need to be reformed to the advantage of small and marginal farmers.

For providing appropriate marketing facilities, along with the transfer of superior technology and assured supply of inputs, contract farming is advocated. Contract farming is not a new innovation in Indian agriculture; it was introduced decades ago by sugar factories in both the private and cooperative sectors, and later by milk unions. The recent interest evinced in contract farming by the private sector should be encouraged. However, fair terms have to be ensured for the contracting parties and an effective adjudication mechanism must be established.

To conclude, in view of the existing institutional arrangements for risk mitigation and marketing, it will be advisable to 'hasten slowly' as far as the introduction of high-value market-oriented crops on small and marginal holdings is concerned. The emphasis should be on strengthening enterprises such as dairying and poultry, which ensure the fuller use of their resources, and for which marketing facilities are reasonably well developed and well accepted by this category of farmers. Of course, the marginal farmers on the fringes of towns, who do practise intensive farming of fruits and vegetables, should be supported in their efforts to develop these activities in more efficient ways. As a rule, for this highly vulnerable group, the strategy for diversification should be guided by the norm of 'from the familiar to the less familiar'.

Non-farm Employment

Even with the introduction of all the measures described above, a large number of the marginal farmers will not be able to subsist on land. It is important to accord the highest importance to non-farm employment in any strategy addressed to improve the lot of the small and marginal farmers. An obvious avenue to increase non-farm employment is to strengthen the natural resource base of Indian farming. There is enough scope to use labour-intensive methods for strengthening land and water resources. Ingenuity, however, lies in designing ways to make people who benefit from these improvements to pay for the benefits. The recently introduced National Employment Guarantee Programme (NEGP) provides an excellent opportunity to offer gainful employment to marginal farmers along with landless workers, while at the same time strengthening the land and water resources in the rural areas. Meanwhile the scope for a massive programme of rural industrialisation should be recognised. With the participation of large farmers, and technical and institutional support offered by relevant agencies at the taluka and district levels, a demand-driven programme of rural industrialisation should be mounted in all earnestness. We can learn valuable lessons in this regard from the Chinese experience, wherein the break-up of the communes into small peasant holdings (the average size of these holdings was less than one-third of the average size of holdings in India) led to a spurt in non-farm activities. The main reason for the growth of non-farm activities in China was the fact that, along with introduction of the 'Household Responsibility System', severe price distortions in agricultural produce were removed to a considerable extent. Both these developments provided the needed incentive to boost agricultural productivity, which was already quite high, especially in comparison to India. With a rise in production and better prices, the cash income of the farmers also increased significantly, leading to an upsurge in their demand for non-farm goods and services. Other factors were also responsible for the phenomenal growth of the non-farm sector in China; the most important among them being a much higher investment in human resources, including education and health, which preceded the institution of the Household Responsibility System. Also, much more effective technological support was available to the small peasant holdings. However, the main reason was the strong demand-induced linkages forged between the agricultural and non-agricultural sectors (Vyas, 2002b).

In India, nothing of that sort happened. The income, particularly cash income, of majority of the cultivators remained abysmally low. Naturally, they could not provide markets for non-agricultural goods and services, which was possible only for the rural rich. Additionally, goods with high capital and high import components dominate their consumption pattern, as in the case of richer sections of the urban population. It is not surprising that such goods find an expanding market in the rural areas, while the rural arts and crafts languish. For the survival of the latter, several other pre-conditions have to be fulfilled, such as better quality, reduced cost, institutional support, infrastructure development, etc., but the most important component in reviving rural non-farm activities would be an hike in the income of the large mass of small and marginal farmers.

Improvements in Delivery Systems

The small farm groups are potentially viable in most of the ecological regions in our country, provided institutional support is made available to them in terms of extension, credit, marketing and risk mitigation. An important ingredient of the new agricultural strategy should be strengthening of the institutional base to support small farm agriculture. The objective of the New Agriculture is not simply to perpetuate a smallholdings agrarian structure, but also to make small farms economically viable, surplus-generating entities. A vibrant small farm agriculture will depend heavily on institutional support. Reforming the delivery systems in order to make them congruent with small farm agriculture is as important as reforms in the land and lease markets. State policies in this, as in other respects, should be consciously designed to support the small farm system. Policies for strengthening the delivery system have to grapple with the twin realities of growing sophistication in marketing and processing of agricultural produce, on one hand, and the need for peoples' participation on the other. In view of the existing and the emergent agrarian structure, action needs to be taken in the following directions:

- De-bureaucratisation of the cooperative and other voluntary organisations; adapting the functioning of large delivery institutions, e.g., in credit, input supply, etc., to the reality of small-scale agriculture.
- Integrating various functions such as input supply, extension and quality control, and more importantly, processing and marketing with larger organisations in a vertical manner.
- Developing effective monitoring and information systems for the large and sophisticated secondary and apex organisations to ensure transparency and accountability.

Creating and Strengthening Farmer's Organisations

Three main arguments are advanced to explain ineffectiveness of the delivery systems *vis-à-vis* small and marginal farmers. These are: (i) high transaction cost, (ii) high risk and (iii) low absorptive capacity.

All these suggest the need for collective organisation of the recipients. In the Indian circumstances, homogeneous groups of agricultural producers with joint liability and catering to multiple needs—not merely the credit requirements—can provide an effective foundation for an efficient and equitable agrarian structure. The rapidly spreading SHG (self-help group) movement has paved the way for this type of organisation, and joint liability groups now need to be introduced into the small farm sector.

Concluding Remarks

The time is now ripe for planning a new agrarian system with a vibrant small farm base on the lines suggested above. With several favourable factors, such as adequate financial resources generated by a fast-growing economy; a vast institutional network for research, extension, credit and marketing; availability of a large number of trained people; improved infrastructure of roads and communication; and relevant experience in our country and in other similarly placed countries of the region in effective farmers' organisations, we can launch bold initiatives in favour of the millions of marginal farmers who have been left out of the mainstream of development to their as well as the country's disadvantage.

References

Ali, Ifzal, B.M. Desai, R. Radhakrishna and V.S. Vyas (1981). "Indian Agriculture at 2000: Strategies for Equity", *Economic and Political Weekly* 16(10, 11 and 12), March.

Bhalla, Sheila (2005). "India: Rural Economy, Issues and Evidence", *Working Paper Series* no.25. New Delhi: Institute for Human Development.

Chadha, G.K. and P.P. Sahu (2005). "Rural Industrialisation in India: Critical Assessment of Policy Perspectives", in Rohini Nayyar and Alakh N. Sharma (eds.), *Rural Transformation in India: The Role of the Non-farm Sector*. New Delhi: Institute for Human Development.

Dantwala, M.L. and C.H. Shah (1971). *Evaluation of Land Reforms*. General Report. Bombay, University of Bombay.

Sen, Abhijit and Himanshu (2004). "Poverty and Inequality in India", *Economic and Political Weekly* 39.

Srivastava, Ravi and Richa Singh (2006). "Rural Wages During the 1990s: A Re-estimation", *Economic and Political Weekly* 41(38).

Vyas, V.S. (1991). "Agrarian Structure, Environmental Concerns and Rural Poverty", *Elmhurst Memorial Lecture*. XXI International Conference of Agricultural Economists, Tokyo, Japan.

———. (1996). "Diversification of Agriculture and Food Security in the Context of New Economic Policy: Concept, Rationale and Approaches", *Indian Journal of Agricultural Economics* 52(4), October-December.

———. (2002a). "Changing Contours of Indian Agriculture", in Rakesh Mohan (ed.), *Facets of the Indian Economy*. New Delhi: Oxford University Press.

———. (2002b). "Our Agrarian Future: A Medium Term Perspective on Asian Agriculture", Presidential Address to the *Fourth Conference of Asian Society of Agricultural Economists*.

Vyas, V.S. and Surjit Singh (2006). "Crop Insurance in India", *Economic and Political Weekly* 41(43 and 44), 4-10 November.

6

Agrarian Distress

*Strategies to Protect Vulnerable Sections**

I

The latest official statistics on poverty (1999-2000) suggest that nearly 26 per cent of our population is BPL (below poverty line). Non-official estimates generally suggest a much higher proportion. Practically all estimates of poverty, official or non-official, indicate that incidence of income poverty is more in rural areas than in the urban areas, and this difference has persisted over time. Translated into the number of BPL people, even on the basis of official estimates, nearly 193 million of the rural people in our country are poor. According to another estimate, the figure could be as high as 209.4 million (Sen and Himanshu, 2003). For a country which is aiming at poverty alleviation for the last 50 years or more, these are not, to say the least, comforting figures.

Apart from the relatively large proportion of households suffering from low incomes, rural households also suffer from deprivations in terms of education and health. The discrepancy is much wider when it comes to the girl child. The indicators such as life expectancy, infant and child mortality, and child malnutrition are appallingly high. It can be safely presumed that the incidence of all such deprivations is more severe among the rural poor.

A worrisome feature is the addition of the 'new poor' among agricultural households. Thanks to an alert press, which brought to light 'starvation deaths' in some regions and the spate of suicides by farmers in others, agrarian distress has received nationwide publicity.

---

* V.V Giri Memorial Lecture delivered at the Conference of Indian Society of Labour Economics organised at Institute of Development Studies, Jaipur, 2004.

However, only partial explanations are offered and ad hoc solutions advanced to deal with the malady. A more systematic treatment is needed to understand the phenomenon of the vulnerable sections of agricultural producers not only in the regions traditionally known as 'backward' regions, but also in other parts of the country.

Considering the painstaking research of several scholars, we have a fairly good knowledge of the contours of what is called, chronic poverty (Sundaram and Tendulkar, 2003; Mehta and Shah, 2004; Mahendra Dev, 2004). There is a large concentration of the chronically poor in certain regions. Over 70 per cent of India's poor are located in six states, i.e., undivided Uttar Pradesh (UP), Bihar, Madhya Pradesh (MP), Maharashtra, West Bengal (WB) and Odisha. While these states together account for roughly half of India's population, the first three states account for approximately 36 per cent of the total population, but 48 per cent of the poor. Households depending on agricultural labour, small and marginal farmers, and rural artisans constitute the bulk of the rural poor. Slightly less than half (48%) of the rural poor are agricultural labourers and more than a quarter (28%) are self-employed in agriculture. Among the social groups, the SCs (scheduled castes) and STs (scheduled tribes), particularly the latter, account for a proportionately larger number of the poor. The same is true about women-headed households. Within the households, women and the elderly suffer greater deprivations.

Apart from the chronically poor, a large number of non-poor households are vulnerable. They can easily slip into the category of the poor due to different types of 'shocks.' The 'push' can come from personal tragedy, e.g., disease and death of the earning member, loss of assets due to natural disasters, or loss of livelihood, or severe impact on the current income due to market-induced factors. If any of these factors persist for long, a household with a thin asset base and without the advantage of a safety net would join the ranks of the chronic poor. Too much should not, therefore, be made of the distinction between chronic and transitory distress. Factors causing transitory distress can aggravate the plight of households already suffering from chronic distress. Similarly, if transitory distress persists over a period of time, it can then lead to a state of chronic distress.

It is important that while attention should be focused on alleviating chronic poverty, measures should be taken to protect the vulnerable sections—in fact, to help them to have a more sustainable household economy. In this connection, it may be useful to distinguish between the risk an individual household faces, i.e., idiosyncratic risk, and that faced by a large number of households, i.e., systemic risk. The latter is mainly due to natural disasters or market-induced 'shocks'. It needs to be pointed out at the outset that shocks of various type may reinforce each other. Households prone to natural disasters may suffer from market shocks as well, which would worsen their plight. Also, a household level disability may further sap the capacity to withstand a market-induced or natural calamity. I shall, however, concentrate on the market-induced systemic risks.

II

Indian agriculture has undergone some major structural changes in recent years, and this has enhanced the market-induced vulnerability of a section of the rural population. Over a period of time, Indian agriculture has been progressively acquiring the 'small farm' character. By 1995-96, nearly 36 per cent of the cultivated area was operated by small and marginal farmers—an increase from the 29 per cent in 1985-86 (Table 6.1). I have analysed the causes for changes in the agrarian structure elsewhere (Vyas, 2002). It can be safely assumed that over 40 per cent of the land is now operated by small and marginal farmers. Such a tilt towards small farms could be observed practically in all parts of the country. With a meagre asset base, a large part of our agriculture is unable to withstand even minor shocks.

There have been significant changes in the output mix in agriculture. These changes are reflected in a shift of area from foodgrains to non-foodgrains, and within foodgrains from coarse cereals to finer cereals. During the last quarter century, the area under foodgrains has declined by over 10 per cent. The move from non-foodgrains to foodgrains is witnessed in all major states of India, with the exception of Punjab and UP (Table 6.2). The decline in the area under coarse cereals is even more steep and is a ubiquitous phenomenon. The land vacated by cereals is occupied by oilseeds, cotton, tobacco and sugar cane. By their very nature, these crops are mainly for sale in the market. Whatever changes take place in prices of these crops affect the farmers very profoundly.

Table 6.1

Area Operated by Operational Holdings

(Area million hectares)

Category of Farmers	*1980-81*	*1985-86*	*1990-91*	*1995-96*
Marginal (less than 1 ha)	19.73	22.04	24.89	28.12
Small (1.0 to 2.0 ha)	23.17	25.71	28.82	30.72
Semi-medium (2.0 to 4.0 ha)	34.65	36.67	38.37	38.95
Medium (4.0 to 10.0 ha)	48.54	47.14	44.75	41.39
Large (10.0 ha and above)	37.71	33	28.65	24.16
All holdings	163.8	164.56	165.48	163.35

Source: *Indian Agriculture in Brief* (various issues) and *Agricultural Statistics at a Glance 2003.*

A similar change, in fact a more far-reaching change, has taken place in the input structure. It is mainly influenced by the spread of modern technology and the relative prices of different inputs. Inputs such as fertilisers, insecticides, mechanical power and improved seeds occupy a prominent place in the input structure. They have substituted organic manure, animal power and farm-retained seeds. The purchase of inputs claims a large share of farmers' cash expenditure. Wherever more 'progressive' agriculture is practised, e.g., GM (genetically modified) cotton, the proportion of input costs, and consequently the current outlay on inputs, go up. The value of inputs, which was ₹55,401 crore in 1993-94, rose to ₹1,03,555 crore in 1999-2000, i.e., by two times. The farmers have to take recourse to credit to a larger extent than in the past for the purchase of these inputs (Table 6.3).

Another major change since the early 1990s has been the growing openness of the economy. At the domestic level, several steps have been taken to free the movement of agricultural commodities and ensure free trade. Licensing requirements have been relaxed, movement restrictions have been lifted, selective credit control has been abolished, and a model marketing act is proposed to allow farmers to bypass the mandatory requirement of sale in regulated markets. Several other measures in the direction of liberalising the domestic markets have been proposed. There are still a number of restrictions and constraints, but the direction in which agricultural economy is moving is clear.

Table 6.2

Area under Foodgrains in Different States to Total Cropped Area (Triennium Ending 1975-76 and Triennium Ending 2001-02)

States	*TE 1976*	*TE 2002*	*Difference*
Odisha	84.40	63.20	-21.20
Kerala	30.90	12.20	-18.70
Andhra Pradesh (AP)	72.60	55.60	-17.00
West Bengal	85.60	70.00	-15.60
Gujarat	46.40	32.10	-14.30
Rajasthan	74.50	60.60	-13.90
Maharashtra	70.30	59.40	-10.90
Tamil Nadu	67.50	59.90	-7.60
Haryana	76.30	70.90	-5.40
Jammu & Kashmir (J&K)	87.80	82.60	-5.20
Assam	73.70	69.30	-4.40
Himachal Pradesh	90.00	86.80	-3.20
Karnataka	65.10	62.30	-2.80
Punjab	68.20	77.00	8.80
UP	72.60	80.60	8.00
All India	74.40	64.30	-10.10

Source: Centre for Monitoring Indian Economy (CMIE), Agriculture, February 2004.

A similar trend in liberalising external trade policies can be discerned, especially from the beginning of 1990s. With the signing of the World Trade Organization (WTO) agreements, this trend has been further strengthened. Quantitative import restrictions have been relaxed, and the list of commodities canalised through state trading enterprises has been trimmed. Import tariff on most commodities has been brought down. Export policies are being progressively liberalised. Thus, at the international plane, the gradual removal of protectionist measures and the slow but progressive integration with a global economy are discernible. These developments obviously expose Indian farmers to the vagaries of not only the domestic markets, but also to price fluctuations at the international level.

Table 6.3

Value of Inputs, Output and Flow of Production Credit in Agriculture at Current Prices

(₹ crore)

Year	*Value of Output Agriculture*	*Value of Input Agriculture*	*Flow of SAO Credit*
1993-94	204874	55401	9752
1994-95	236607	63654	11932
1995-96	256698	72026	15273
1996-97	302744	74415	16956
1997-98	319586	83125	18632
1998-99	387546	93005	20601
1999-2000	405576	103555	23694

Source: Rural Credit and NABARD 2003 (for value of output from agriculture) and National Accounts Statistics 2001 (for value of input from agriculture).

III

These changes are taking place at a time when the rate of growth in agricultural production is decelerating. Careful analysis by scholars has shown that the productivity gains achieved during 1970s and 1980s could not be sustained in the last decade (Deshpande *et al.*, 2004). The process of deceleration in the growth of agriculture had started in 1990s, when the agricultural growth rate came down to less than 2.4 per cent, from 3.8 per cent per annum in the previous decade. Except for one year, 2003-04, the downward slide has continued. The average agricultural GDP growth in the first two years of the Tenth Plan was 1.8 per cent. It is likely to be 1.5 per cent in the third year. The declining trend in productivity, as signified by the yield per hectare, is more disturbing. The deceleration in yields has been witnessed in practically all crops and in a majority of regions. In fact, there was virtual stagnation in the yields of 'commercial crops' during 1990s with sugar cane registering less than 1 per cent growth in yield per year, and cotton and tobacco witnessing negative growth. The serious drought years in the earlier part of this decade has had a part in accentuating the decline, but the factors causing distress to agriculture are more abiding.

Deceleration in productivity has to be viewed in the context of the rising share of purchased inputs, especially in 'commercial' crops. A number of studies at the state level, as well as the micro level, have shown that once the use of fertilisers crosses the 'low utilisation level', diminishing return starts. It is even more true in the case of pesticides (Venugopal, 2004; Birthal, 2004). The plight of the growers has been compounded because of not only the declining trend in yield from inputs, but also output prices of agricultural commodities, especially of the commercial crops, remaining subdued in the last few years. As a result, the terms of trade (Index of Prices Received divided by Index of Prices Paid) remained stable during the last five years, hovering around 103-105 in contrast to a rising trend in the previous decade. Recent years have also witnessed much larger fluctuations in the output prices around a mildly declining trend. The net result has been that Indian agriculturists face lower returns and larger uncertainty.

Obviously, not all growers in all regions faced a similar situation. There were groups of producers who benefited from state policies on pricing and subsidies. There were also pockets where productivity growth could be sustained (Sen and Bhatia, 2004). But the fact that, on an average, the situation on both price and productivity levels was depressed suggests that in terms of loss of income, some groups have suffered more than what is reflected in the average decline in prices and output. These are the vulnerable groups—mainly, farmers in dry land areas, agricultural labourers, marginal and small farmers all over the country, and commercial farmers who went in for heavy doses of purchased inputs—to whom we should now pay larger attention.

IV

During this difficult period, policy interventions and institutional support to agriculture proved to be grossly inadequate. Policy failure was reflected in much larger emphasis on prices and subsidies than on non-price productivity, augmenting factors such as research, extension and investment in infrastructure. The way the administered price regime was unfolding in the last few years, it was clear that policymakers were using prices as vehicles for transferring income rather than as signals for resource allocation. Indiscriminate use of subsidies, particularly input subsidies, crowded out the resources for public investment in infrastructure (Vyas, 2002).

Measures to contain risks also proved ineffective and in certain cases, counterproductive. Basically, three types of measures were taken for mitigation of risks. The MSP (minimum support price) was used to minimise market-induced risks, with a guarantee to purchase all the output at pre-announced prices. With the emphasis on covering all the costs of farming, actual as well as imputed, and their operation largely restricted to a limited number of crops—mainly rice, wheat and sugar cane—MSP contributed to a greater distortion in the cropping patterns rather than proving itself an effective shield for the agriculturists. The second measure to mitigate risks was crop insurance. In actual practice, it has proved to be of marginal support only in some regions (e.g., Gujarat) and for some crops (e.g., groundnuts and paddy). A measure to insure income in the face of market-induced risks as well as decline in yield due to natural causes is being introduced as a pilot project in a few districts for a few crops. There is a National Fund for Calamity Relief, with a limited objective of providing relief to victims of natural calamities. Its operations during the last five years could provide assistance to 10 per cent of the requests made by the states. Although there is a renewed emphasis on forward markets, they have yet to make a substantial presence. In sum, we do not have an effective policy for minimising uncertainty or providing strength to farmers so as to withstand natural and market-induced risks.

Institutional failures are even more glaring. In the present context, the two most relevant institutions are extension and credit institutions. With one of the world's largest extension systems, one would have expected that all sections of farmers to receive timely and proper advice on and support for the adoption of an appropriate enterprise and technology mix. In fact, the role of the extension institutions in acting as a conduit between the scientists and users is practically non-existent. There are a few instances of private enterprises entering the field of extension of technology in raising crops and animal husbandry. However, the main source of information on modern inputs are the input suppliers who have a field day in 'educating' farmers in the use of purchased inputs. They naturally have a vested interest in increasing the use of inputs they might be dealing in, irrespective of their impact on productivity. Studies at the ground level from all parts of the country, and more so from the regions where input use is increasing rapidly, suggest that there is a disproportionate use of all inputs on the farms, leading to increased liability of the farmers. The blame for the suicides of agriculturists in some parts of the country can be, at least partly, attributed to the failure of the extension agencies who could not check spurious inputs or guide the farmers in the proper use of inputs.

Another major handicap faced by the farming community is in the functioning of credit institutions in the formal sector, i.e., RFIs (rural financial institutions). It is quite clear that RFIs are not advancing credit to agriculture at the rate warranted by the increased requirement of credit with the larger use of purchased inputs. Some of the poorest parts of the country, e.g., the tribal belt extending from Jharkhand to Andhra Pradesh and encompassing tribal areas of Bihar, Odisha, Maharashtra and Chhattisgarh, are inadequately served by RFIs. Even in the other agriculturally advanced areas, the share of credit from RFIs in the total cost of inputs is low, and there is no indication of the gap being filled. RFIs, particularly commercial banks, advance three reasons for their unsatisfactory performance in rural areas. These are: (1) low absorptive capacity in rural areas, (2) high transaction costs, and (3) greater risks. Only recently as a member of two different committees, I have had the opportunity to examine the functioning of RFIs in detail.[1] I have more to say on these aspects a little later.

With the reluctance and/or inability of RFIs, farmers have to take recourse to non-formal sources, i.e., input suppliers, traders and bigger landlords, to obtain credit. While it may be easy to get credit from these sources, it is also true that the terms they offer are onerous;

1. Expert Committee on Rural Credit (Chairman: V.S. Vyas), National Bank for Agriculture and Rural Development (NABARD), Mumbai, 2002. Advisory Committee on the Flow of Credit to Agriculture (Chairman: V.S. Vyas, Reserve Bank of India [RBI]), Mumbai, 2004.

their methods of recovery could also be more ruthless. Farmers who are heavily indebted to these sources, but unable to generate additional output, and therefore default in repayment, face severe consequences. It is no coincidence that the largest number of suicides are reported from areas where farmers get heavily indebted to non-formal sources of credit.

Declining growth rates in production, stagnant prices and high cost of production have hit the agricultural sector as a whole. There are certain sections of the agricultural population which have fared worse than others. The more important among them are the agricultural producers in dry areas. Large parts of Gujarat, Rajasthan, Maharashtra and Odisha fall in this category. With depleted land resources, low and uncertain rainfall and low prices of their produce, these farmers are worse off even in normal years. Long-term trends in productivity of the crops grown in the dry areas, e.g., coarse cereals and pulses suggest a stagnation in their yields. Their plight is further aggravated as three out of four years of this decade have proved to be 'below normal' in rainfall in large parts of the dry region. Whatever savings they had were depleted during these prolonged dry years. Their capacity to withstand any shock, natural or market-induced, has been completely eroded.

The only saving feature in these regions is the fact that a larger proportion of the holdings are medium to large. But, there are a substantial number of smallholdings as well. In these regions, those with marginal and smallholdings are worse off. As producers, they get paltry returns from their farming which are further affected by adverse weather and market conditions. Generally, these groups also have a subsidiary source of income in dairy and animal husbandry enterprises, which are sustained on open grazing. The depletion of commons as a result of prolonged drought in several areas has made the cattle and other animals more a liability than an asset. Another source of income for these households is farm and non-farm labour. From available evidence, it seems that the employment opportunities have dwindled and there is no commensurate increase in wages (Bhalla, 2004). Severe distress is evident among these groups of small farmers and agricultural labourers, and these categories overlap in dry areas.

The plight of the farmers who have gone the whole hog with diversification is equally distressful. While the former groups, i.e., small and marginal farmers in dry areas, suffer from acute malnutrition and starvation, more of the suicide cases are reported from the groups who have borrowed heavily to purchase inputs for what they thought were more remunerative crops. With the high input-low output scenario described earlier, the result has been failure to repay the loans. As most of these loans were contracted through so-called non-formal sources, who could resort to social pressures as much as coercive tactics, many self-respecting farmers had taken the extreme step of suicide to save face.

V

I will like to suggest three-pronged strategy to save the situation from further deterioration *viz.*,

- Instituting creditable risk mitigating measures
- Investment for strengthening land and water resources
- Strengthening supportive institutions, especially in the areas of extension and credit.

Mitigating risks for the poor: As I have indicated earlier, we have an array of measures to support the poor and mitigate the risks faced by them; more general programmes such as poverty alleviation programmes, and programmes to strengthen backward regions, as well as specific programmes to mitigate risks, such as minimum support prices, crop insurance, the National Calamity Fund, safety nets for indigent and handicapped people, and so on. There is no better indication of their ineffectiveness than the sorry plight of a large section of the rural people (Vyas, 2001).

The principal policy measures to mitigate risks are MSPs and crop insurance. I have pointed out the lacunae in MSP as it operates today. It has offered limited safeguards to a section of producers, mainly wheat and rice growers in selected areas, and has distorted the allocative function of prices and created a strong lobby of rent seekers.

Suggestions have been offered to minimise the damage and improve upon the present policy on MSP (Vyas, 2002). The Income Guarantee Scheme, tried in a few districts, is not a substitute for the ill-managed MSP. It has all the disadvantages of MSP with additional demands on scarce resources.

There is considerable scope in improving our programme of crop insurance. Its coverage has to extend much beyond the limited area and limited number of crops. Eventually, a more comprehensive insurance product has to be offered to the farmers, going beyond crops, and including insurance of animals and equipment, and covering life and health aspects of the rural population. Several of the operational lacunae have to be removed. It should however be clear that, even with all these reforms, we will not be able to recover premia from the rural poor at actuarial rates. An element of subsidy is inevitable. This is the type of subsidy for which there is full justification on grounds of both equity and efficiency.

As far as natural risks are concerned, the farmers in the risk-prone areas have devised their own coping mechanisms. These involve self-provisioning on one hand and diversification to supplementary and complementary enterprises on the other. Generally, mixed crops, dominated by cereals (the major source of calories) and pulses (major source of protein), characterise the cropping pattern in dry regions, especially on small farms. And animal husbandry—dairying mainly—is the major supplementary occupation. In our anxiety to introduce 'high value' agriculture, this pattern is being discouraged, without extending assured food supply through, say PDS, and without ensuring institutional support in marketing and credit for the new crops. In the absence of these supportive measures, we are exposing the vulnerable farmers of dry areas to a high-risk environment. This may not apply to small farmers on the fringe of cities and towns for whom a ready market for fruits, vegetables and other high-value crops exist. The uncertainty faced by them arises more due to sharp price fluctuations.

In this context, contract farming is suggested as a way out. Certainly, if properly implemented, contract farming arrangements can mitigate at least the market-induced risks. Contract farming is not new to India. We have a long tradition of contract farming, particularly in sugar and to a large extent in milk. Experience has shown that in areas where contract farming is organised in the cooperative mode, with a major say of the producers at all stages in the value chain, it has not only contributed in improving productivity on the growers' farms, but has also ensured them an assured income and a larger share of the consumer's rupee. Contract farming with the involvement of large private firms as collaborators has shown mixed results, with more failures than successes. Problems of moral hazard and adverse selection are rampant, and complaints about inadequate guidance in input use and farm practices as well as non-enforcement of contracts are voiced frequently.

In the present circumstances, the thrust of the policy should be on encouraging improvement in the productivity of crops grown in dry regions and on small farms—mainly coarse cereals, pulses and *kharif* oilseeds. Measures to encourage productivity in the dairy sector is equally important for these groups. These regions can have a comparative advantage in dairying based on open grazing due to large areas of cultivable wasteland and 'goucher' land, provided a massive programme of land development is taken up. Only when the small farmers broadly reach their self-sufficiency level, and start generating surpluses from their traditional crops and enterprises, should diversification to input-intensive, high-value crops and enterprises be encouraged. Our immediate task should be to encourage self-provisioning, rather than market exposure, as far as small and marginal farmers are concerned.

Investment in strengthening land and water resources: Since the mid-1980s, public investment in agriculture has progressively declined. Nor has private investment been able to fill the gap. As a result, total capital formation in agriculture is decelerating. The bulk of investment made in both public and private sectors is accounted for by investment in augmenting irrigation resources; in the case of public investment, it is canal irrigation, and in case of private investment, it is in groundwater exploitation. Due to a lack of complementary investment in operations and maintenance and bureaucratic handling of this resource use, the efficiency of canal water is seriously jeopardised. On the other hand, concentration of private investment in groundwater exploitation has resulted in over-exploitation of the resource leading to negative externalities in several regions of the country, especially in the arid and semi-arid areas where progressively larger areas are coming under the 'dark zone'.

In any strategy for protecting the vulnerable sections in agriculture, augmentation, conservation and efficient use of water should receive high priority. This would involve larger and more imaginatively planned investment, much greater collaboration between irrigation engineers and agricultural scientists, policy support to ensure equitable distribution and recovery of irrigation dues. In all these measures, the role of water-users and the civil society institutions will be critical.

There is growing recognition of the inadequacies of our efforts in augmenting and rejuvenating land resources. However, it is yet to be translated in terms of investment and policy packages. The severity of the problem can be gauged by the fact that, according to the Ministry of Agriculture, Government of India, more than 42 per cent of the geographical area of the country comprises degraded land. A substantial part of it is manmade. The extent of degraded land is, again, higher in the states with a larger share of rainfed agriculture. Remedial measures to rejuvenate these lands have not gone beyond tokenism. Investment in land development, by both public and private initiatives, should receive serious attention. Failure to take credible action to stop the process of degradation and develop the degraded lands would mean that the natural resource base of our agriculture will be progressively weakened, and the incidence will fall more seriously on the backward regions and vulnerable sections of agricultural producers.

Strengthening supportive institutions: In any scheme for reducing vulnerability of the poorer sections, especially small and marginal farmers, institutional support in research, extension, credit and marketing is of paramount importance. We have in this country a wide network of institutions working in these areas. However, there is such incongruence between the service delivery systems and the bulk of the poor in rural areas, mostly accounted for by the small and marginal farmers, that the latter hardly gets any support from them. For example, research and extension institutions bypass them as any improvement on their tiny holdings is not likely to make much difference at the macro level. In any case, because of the thin asset base, the capacity of these sections to face uncertainty is considered to be limited. Credit and marketing institutions find that the demands placed by these sections on the service providers are infrequent and in small bits. This makes the transaction costs heavy and uneconomical.

There are ways to cope with these difficulties and create a supportive institutional framework for the disadvantaged sections. Scaling up of their operations through cooperative effort has proved to be a viable solution, as the experience of SHGs, now numbering nearly eight million, in dispersal and recovery of credit has convincingly demonstrated. An example of the successful interface between small producers and marketing institutions is provided by the dairy cooperatives, which have enabled an owner of one or two buffaloes to get the benefits of advanced and appropriate technology. The scope for institutional support can be further enhanced by making proper use of information technology. There are numerous models of institutional interventions to benefit marginalised groups. These models have to be adapted and extended to meet with specific requirements in different settings.

To provide immediate redress to the affected peasantry, measures to give relief to those heavily indebted to the private moneylenders and traders are urgently needed. A proposal was made, long back, to restrict the total amount of interest due to the value of the sum initially borrowed, popularly known as the principle of Dam Duppat. This has to be enacted as a legislation and made applicable retrospectively. Similarly, the legislation prohibiting usurious moneylending should be made effective in all the states. A measure of similar intent would be to encourage RFIs to take over loans contracted by the farmers from private sources on their books. Waiving of interest or even the principal amount borrowed from RFIs will not help much, unless steps are taken to lighten the burden of those who have contracted large amounts from non-formal sources.

VI

We have a serious problem on hand because of the growing vulnerability of large sections of the rural population. It is possible, however, to turn the tide by

- enhancing investment in strengthening the resource base of agriculture,
- by devising suitable instruments to protect, in any event to compensate small and marginal producers for losses arising from natural calamities,
- by designing organisational interventions to impart strength to their economy,
- by lightening the interest burden from the non-formal sources of credit, and
- by encouraging RFIs to take over debts of the farmers from usurious sources.

A positive feature in our situation is that we have some examples of success in all these directions. There is a need to extend and scale up these efforts.

Present policies and programmes are not able to protect a sizeable section of agricultural population from natural and market-induced uncertainities, nor to enable them to contribute meaningfully to overall growth of the economy. We have a responsibility towards this section of the agricultural population. Making them less vulnerable will not only contribute to social equity, but will also accelerate economic growth. The choice seems clear.

References

Bhalla, G.S. (2004). "Globalisation and Indian Agriculture", New Delhi: Academic Foundation.

Bhalla, Sheila, Anup K. Karan, T. Shobah (2004). "Rural Casual Labourers: Wages and Poverty 1983 to 1999-2000", *Working Paper.* New Delhi: IIPA.

Birthal, Pratap S. (2004). "Integrated Pest Management in Indian Agriculture", *ICAR, Proceedings.* National Centre for Agricultural Economics and Policy Research (NACP) and National Centre for Integrated Pest Management (NCIPM), New Delhi.

Deshpande, R.S., M.J. Bhende, P. Thipaiah, M. Vivekananda (2004). "Crops and Cultivation", *State of Indian Farmers: A Millennium Study.* New Delhi: Academic Foundation.

Mahendra Dev, S. (2004). "Is Rural India Shinning", *Working Paper* No 54. Hyderabad: Centre for Economic and Social Studies.

Mehta, Aasha Kapur and Amita Shah (2004). "Chronic Poverty in India: An Overview", *Working Paper.* New Delhi: IIPA.

National Bank for Agriculture and Rural Development (2002). *Expert Committee on Rural Credit* (Chairman, V.S. Vyas).

Reserve Bank of India (2004). *Report of the Advisory Committee on Flow of Credit to Agriculture and Related Activities from the Banking System* (Chairman V.S. Vyas).

Sen, Abhijit and Himanshu (2003). "Poverty and Inequality in India: Getting Close to the Truth". New Delhi: Centre for Economics Studies and Planning, Jawaharlal Nehru University. *Mimeo.*

Sen, Abhijit and M.S. Bhatia (2004). "Cost of Cultivation and Farm Income", in *State of Indian Farmers: A Millennium Study.* New Delhi: Academic Foundation.

Sundaram, K. and S.D. Tendulkar (2003). "Poverty in India in the 1990s: Revised Results", *Economic and Political Weekly* 38(46), November 15.

Venugopal, Pingali (2004). "Input Management", in *State of Indian Farmers: A Millennium Study.* New Delhi: Academic Foundation.

Vyas, V.S. (2001). "Agriculture: Second Round of Economic Reforms", *Economic and Political Weekly* 36(10).

———. (2002). "Changing Contours of Indian Agriculture", in Rakesh Mohan (ed.), *Facets of Indian Economy: The NCAER Golden Jubilee Lectures.* OUP India.

———. (n.d.). "Seven Lessons of Poverty Alleviation Programme", *Mimeo.*

7

Towards an Equitable Agrarian Structure*

In a country where nearly 60 per cent of the workforce depends on agriculture, relationship with land must be considered of primary importance. Access to land determines income and welfare of a large section of the population in the rural areas. More so because access to credit and other inputs is also closely linked to the size of landholding. A time has come to bring back to the centre stage the issues of ownership and access to land in our discussion of rural economy.

In this paper, I will highlight the pattern of landholdings as it prevails in our country, legislations enacted in our country to change the agrarian structure and the limited success they have achieved. I will outline a more equitable and efficient landholding structure and the place of land reforms and land markets in achieving it. My main focus is on the lower end of the holding structure, i.e., the marginal holdings (less than 1 ha).[1] While soil fertility and the location of holdings, hence the income-earning capacity of land, will differ from one region to another, one can safely assume that a holding of less than a hectare will not be an economically viable one under most circumstances. As a large number of households fall under this category, it is important to look into the alternatives that can be provided to them.

---

* 5th Prof Ranjit Gupta Memorial Lecture delievered at BASIX Academy for Livelihood and Micro Banking Practice, Hyderabad, 21 February 2014.

1. In our country, landholdings are generally categorised in the following groups: Marginal holdings with less than 1 ha; small holdings of 1-2 ha; semi-medium holdings 2-4 ha; medium 4-10 ha; and large more than 10 ha. I am following this classification in this text.

I

Agrarian Structure

Dependence on Agriculture: An abiding feature of India's rural scene is an overwhelming dependence on agriculture for livelihood. In rural areas, nearly 80 per cent of the employed males and 87 per cent of the employed females were working in agriculture in the year 1977-78; the proportion of the employed males and females in agriculture in the year 2009-10, the latest year for which we have comparable data, was 63 and 79 respectively. This suggests a shift of less than 1 per cent to non-farm occupations in a year. The situation has not changed in any remarkable way even if we take more recent years, from 1999-2000 to 2009-10.[2]

Composition of Agricultural Workforce: However, the composition of agricultural workforce—between cultivators and agricultural workers—is changing, as is the size distribution of agricultural holdings. Untill 1991, the proportion of agricultural workers in the total agricultural workforce (cultivators + agricultural workers) was increasing only at a slow pace. The picture has changed since then as the proportion of agricultural workers has increased significantly, together with the increase in the marginal farmers. It seems that more and more marginal farmers with small plots of land are opting for agricultural labour as their main occupation. This is reflected in the fact that more than half (56%) of the agricultural labour households possess some land (i.e., between 0.4 and 1 ha).

Distribution of Landholdings: As I have mentioned earlier, the increase in agricultural workforce is mainly due to the fast growth of marginal holdings, which could not provide adequate income to their operators. This process has accelerated in recent years. I have discussed elsewhere major changes that have taken place in the agrarian structure (Vyas, 2009). These can be summarised as follows:

- Proportion of agricultural workers in the agricultural workforce has increased. However, proportion of landless labourers in the

2. Figures quoted in this paper, unless otherwise mentioned, are from the National Sample Survey (NSS) Round 66 (pertaining to July 2009 to June 2010) published by Ministry of Statistics and Programme Implementation, Government of India, November 2011.

total agricultural workers has not increased in any remarkable way; it is the marginal and sub-marginal farmers who are swelling the rank of agricultural labourers.

- Landholding structure in India is sliding downwards, with progressively greater concentration in the marginal holding group.
- Not only is the number of marginal holdings increasing, the area cultivated in marginal holdings is also going up.
- The proportion of area under medium and semi-medium holdings accounts for nearly half of the agricultural area, and has remained more or less constant.
- There has been a significant decline in the number of large holdings as well as area cultivated by them.
- Reported area under tenancy is relatively small—around 8 per cent, although there is large area under concealed tenancy.
- All size-groups of holdings participate as lessor as well as lessee, but small and marginal farmers dominate as tenets.

Increase in Marginal Holdings: Among the salient features of agrarian structure described above, most noteworthy is the increase in the number of and area under marginal holdings. In 2010-11, the latest year for which agricultural census data are available for the country as a whole and for individual states in required details, 92.4 million of the cultivated holdings were in the size group of 1 ha or less. About 35.1 million ha of land was cultivated by this size-group of farmers (Ministry of Agriculture, 2012). Over a period of time, the number of as well as area under cultivation in this size-group of holdings is increasing. In 1970-71, these holdings accounted for 51 per cent of the total cultivated holdings. A decade later, the proportion rose to 56 per cent. The latest census (2010-11) suggests that their share in the total holdings has reached 67 per cent.

It is generally appreciated that a large majority of cultivators in our country are marginal farmers. However, what is noteworthy is the fact that progressively larger share of cultivated land is farmed by this group. In 1970-71, nearly 9 per cent of the land was cultivated in holdings of 1 ha or less. A decade later, the proportion of land cultivated in marginal holdings was 12 per cent of the cultivated area. By 2010-11, their share in the total cultivated land rose to 25 per cent, after excluding holdings of less than 0.4 ha (i.e., 1 acre). Already, by 1995-96, in five states, one-third or more of the cultivated area was in marginal holdings: Kerala (53%), West Bengal (WB) (43%), Jammu and Kashmir (J&K) (40%), Bihar (36%) and Uttar Pradesh (UP) (34%). By 2010-11, the area cultivated by marginal farmers increased in all these states—and one more state, Tamil Nadu (TN), joined the ranks. Thus, marginal farmers not only constitute an overwhelming majority of the cultivators, they are becoming increasingly important as agricultural producers too. There are few states, most notably Punjab, where the area cultivated in marginal holdings has declined.

As against that, the number of and the area under semi-medium holding (2-4 ha) has not changed much. There has been some—less than 2 per cent—decline in the proportion of medium sized holdings (4-10 ha), and slightly greater decline (nearly 3%) in the proportion of area cultivated by them. Most significant decline has been in the number of and area cultivated by large farmers, i.e., those owning 10 ha and above.

Two factors have significantly influenced the changes in the holding pattern, most important being the demographic factor. In the absence of opportunities for non-farm employment, with increase in population, sub-division of agricultural holdings took place to provide some means of sustenance to new entrants. The other contributing factor, more prominent in the past, is surrendering part of their holdings by small and medium farmers to moneylenders in order o repay their debt. In recent years, commercialisation leading to more active land market has also emerged as an important factor, as the small farmers are compelled to sell part of their holdings to make both ends meet, to repay debts, or to meet social obligations. There are few states, most notable among these being Punjab, where the area cultivated in marginal holdings has declined. If gross value of agriculture per hectare of cultivated land is taken as an indicator of commercialisation, generally, then states where there had been a proportionate decline in the share of marginal holdings had high value of agricultural produce per hectare compared to average value in the country as a whole.

Another factor, though a weak one, was the distribution of ceiling-surplus land in small lots of 1 or 2 acres (0.4-0.8 ha). Purchase of small plots of land by landless workers to join the rank of small farmers could have been another reason for swelling of the ranks of the marginal farmers. However, there is no evidence of this happening in a noticeable way in any part of the country.

II

Economy of the Marginal Farmers

By all indications, income from agriculture has improved during the last few years. The production per hectare of major crops has increased, agricultural prices have improved, and the terms of trade have gone in favour of agriculture. However, we cannot assume that all cultivators have gained equitably. Economic gains availed by various sections of the farming population are predicted by extent and quality of land, cropping pattern, and supplementary sources of income, mainly animal husbandry and farm and non-farm labour. Some sections, i.e., those who have large and better quality of land, easier access to inputs, especially credit, and are growing high-value crops, have fared better in this process. Others, especially the marginal farmers, are left behind, more so in dry, rainfed areas. This group sustains itself mainly on what they can produce from their land, together with two other important activities, *viz.*, agricultural labour and animal husbandry.

Clearly, the quality of land resources in terms of yield potential can compensate for the small size of holding. If we take irrigated area as an indicator of more productive land, small and marginal farmers seem to be in an advantageous position. At the aggregate level, small farmers have larger proportion of area under irrigation, and as a result, they have a higher cropping intensity. They have to, however, rely more on flow irrigation, largely on the public irrigation system. With deceleration in the expansion of flow irrigation and deterioration in quality of irrigation infrastructure, the advantage which this group had in regard to assured water supply is fast disappearing. On the other hand, irrigation from groundwater sources is continuously increasing, presumably on the medium and large farms.

Whatever evidence is available suggests that low-value cereals and other food crops dominate the cropping pattern on these holdings (Sen and Bhatia, 2004). Basic logic for growing low-value food crops rests on the need for self-provisioning, low input requirements and low family labour employment (latter as the alternative wage-paid employment, is needed to earn cash). With low and inefficient penetration of the PDS (public distribution system) and lack of access to credit and institutional support in extension and marketing, this approach to crop planning has full justification. A shift to high-value crops, e.g., fruits and vegetables, can relax the limitation imposed by small size of holdings.

However, these high-value crops need efficient marketing, higher share of purchased inputs and entail higher risk. Only a small section among the marginal farmers, such as vegetable growers at the fringe of urban areas, can satisfy these conditions.

By all indications, marginal farmers are faced with the prospects of raising low-value crops. Even if the yields of these crops on their holdings could be raised to a realistic level, with the limitations imposed by meagre land resources, it is doubtful whether or not their economic status can improve substantially (Ali *et al.*, 1980). Two other options, i.e., wage labour and dairy, seem to be more promising for this section of cultivators.

Agriculture labour is an important and, for many households in this category, the main source of income. Earnings from agricultural labour depend on the days of employment and the wages. Available studies suggest that the period of employment in cultivation is shrinking, because of curtailment of net cultivated area, swift pace of mechanisation (e.g., in Punjab and Haryana) or change over to less labour-intensive cropping patterns (as in Kerala). Rising number of agricultural labourers, coupled with fuller employment of the family labour, especially of women have expanded the pool of labour. In sum, elasticity of employment with respect to output growth in agriculture is approaching near zero level.

Trends in agricultural wages suggest that there has been an increase in the real wages of agricultural labour during the last decade. The increase in real wages has been uneven, with more progressive regions registering higher wages. (It may be a reason why the growth of marginal holdings in the prosperous regions is slower.) Female labour did not benefit to the extent that male labour did. With increase in the proportion of casual labour, uncertainty with regard to wage earnings increased. In any event, marginal farmers 'tied' to their small piece of land cannot avail the benefits of peak season rise in wages.

Another important source of income, particularly for the small and marginal farmers, is Mahatma Gandhi National Rural Employment Guarantee Act (MGNREGA). In 2009-10, about one-third (35%) of rural households had MGNREGA job cards and nearly one-fourth (24%) of rural households got work. A large section of labour working under this scheme is landless labourers and marginal farmers. To the latter, while this provides extra income, it is at the cost of work on their own holdings. Neglect of agriculture on these holdings will adversely impact the income of the marginal farmers. Besides, with more than 25 per cent of cultivated land in these holdings, impact on the agricultural economy of our country will not be insubstantial. This is not to deny the advantages MGNREGA has brought to the agricultural workers by breaking the monopsony power of larger landowners, resulting in higher farm wages.

A major source of income for this group is animal husbandry and poultry. Option of livestock raising (and poultry) is warranted to ensure higher income and employment as also a strategy for risk mitigation. As in the case of landholding structure, important changes are taking place in the animal husbandry sector also. More important among these are: (i) increase in the number of cattle, buffaloes and poultry has slowed down in the 1990s compared to the previous decade; (ii) among bovines, the number of buffaloes is increasing rapidly and the number of in-milk cattle is declining; (iii) there is a positive relationship between in-milk bovine stock and operational holding; larger-sized holdings could maintain larger bovine stock; (iv) there is a marked decrease in the number of working cattle, i.e., bullocks, because of falling importance of bullock power in crop cultivation and allied activities; and (v) a positive feature is the spread of organised marketing in dairy products, especially in cooperative sector.[3]

The marginal holdings also experienced the impact of these changes in the livestock economy. They could retain their share of in-milk bovine stock, rather increased to some extent, but their share in buffaloes, which are emerging as the main dairy animals in the country, has declined. Their share in the bovine stock, in sheep and goats (more so in the latter), has slightly increased, as has been their share in poultry stock. Overall, in the livestock and poultry sectors, marginal farmers are holding their own, except in the more dominant dairy sector, as their capacity to own and maintain the more profitable milch animal, buffalo, puts them in a disadvantageous position.

Other important source of income for workers in the marginal holding group could be wage labour in non-farm occupations. In general, wages in the non-farm sector are higher compared to the farm wages for the country as a whole as well as in most of the states. The real problem is the slow growth in employment opportunities in the non-farm sector.

As was mentioned earlier, there was only a slow process of diversification of the rural economy during the last quarter century or more. The causes as well as consequences of slow growth in rural non-farm sector have been carefully analysed by several scholars. General conclusions emerging from these studies are: sluggish growth in employment in the non-farm sector, which seems to have further slowed down in recent years; among the non-farm activities, relatively higher growth in the tertiary sector, e.g., construction, trade, transport and communication; and fast casualisation of workforce in these sectors in the rural areas. It is reasonable to assume that employment opportunities for marginal farmers in non-farm sector have not increased, except maybe in the construction sector, and the nature of employment is becoming progressively ad hoc and intermittent. The conclusion is inescapable: the plight of a large, rather the largest,

3. See NSS 59th Round, "Land and Livestock Holdings and Debt & Investment", January to December 2003.

section of the rural population, the marginal farmers, has worsened over a period of time.

An aspect of the small-farm-dominated structure, which has not received as much attention as warranted, is its impact on inter-sectoral relationship. It appears that impact of agricultural growth on poverty reduction is weakening over a period of time. Changing agrarian pattern with the ever-increasing weight of small and marginal farmers provides some explanation of this phenomenon. With increase in self-provisioning by this category of farmers, more of the marketable surplus is coming from larger holdings who could take advantage of favourable prices. In the consumption pattern of those (surplus-generating) households, goods and services from organised urban sector dominate. The result is that the impact of agricultural growth on rural poverty is muted.

III

Towards an Equitable Agrarian Structure

As discussed above, the agrarian structure in our country is gradually sliding towards marginal holdings (i.e., holdings with less than 1 ha of cultivated land). If the present trend persists, attenuation of cultivated holdings will continue in the coming years and the number of marginal holdings as well as area operated by them will increase. As I have shown earlier, a large proportion of these marginal farmers is subsisting on wage-paid labour, though they continue to hold their tiny piece of land, more for security reasons rather than as a source of income.

Although with declining importance of land and growing importance of the non-land inputs in agriculture, the size of the holding is not the decisive criterion for remunerative farming, it can be safely assumed that barring some exceptional circumstances, the 'handkerchief holdings,' say of less than a hectare, will not be economically viable. Our objective should be to create as many viable farms as possible.

It is erroneous to conclude from above that large-scale, estate farming is the better alternative. There is enough evidence to suggest that large holdings, apart from their socially disruptive role, do not have any intrinsic advantage in crop production (Sen and Bhatia, 2004). In present circumstances, semi-medium (holdings of 2-4 ha) and medium holdings (4-10 ha) are viable in most of the regions. We should aim at an agrarian structure characterised by semi-medium and medium sized holdings.

To achieve objectives of such an equitable and efficient agriculture structure, a three-pronged strategy suggests:

- increase the land base of marginal and small farmers,
- improve productivity and value addition on these farms, and
- increase the scope for off-farm employment for marginal farmers.

It needs to be emphasised that these elements of the proposed strategy are not distinct alternatives; in most of the situations, they can be made complementary to each other. Also, this strategy will succeed to the extent supportive institutions for research, extension, marketing and credit assist the emerging structure, and small farmers are organised to obtain better bargaining position. On this occasion, I will mainly discuss first of the three elements of the proposed strategy, i.e., scope for expanding the land base of the small farmers.

Expanding the land base: An asset of the small and marginal farmers, which distinguishes them from other marginalised sections of rural population, is their land. It can be postulated that in most regions of the country, holdings below 2 ha, especially those below 1 ha, are non-viable. There is a 'floor' below which agriculture will not be profitable even in the most favourable conditions. (This is indicated by the fact that in the lowest categories of landholdings, there is larger area owned than operated). We should explore possibilities of expanding land base of the marginal farmers, in other words, to provide them a 'ladder' to reach higher landholding category, or provide them alternative employment opportunities.

An important strategy to enhance holding size of the marginal farmers and provide land to the landless rural labourers is land reforms, especially the ceiling on landholdings and distribution of surplus land. Let me briefly review the nature and content of land reforms legislated and implemented in our country.

Earlier Phase of Land Reforms: In the years preceding and immediately following Independence, significant measures of land reforms were undertaken. This was mainly because functionless intermediaries controlled a large part of land; and skewness in landholding pattern was worsening. Even in *ryotwari* areas, layers of intermediaries enjoying various rights, but hardly any obligation, were rampant. Due to the plethora of tenures and several rungs of the intermediaries, relationship to the land had become very complex and litigation was thriving. The first set of land reform legislations was aimed at correcting this situation. Although land reform is a state subject, owing to a national consensus on the direction of land reforms, actual legislation followed more or less the same content and sequence throughout the country. Practically in all states of the country, the reforms proceeded in following stages:

- Abolition of functionless intermediaries (such as *zamindars* and *jagirdars*).
- Protection of tenants' rights and regulation of rent.
- Legislation aimed at 'land to the tiller'.
- Ceiling on landholdings and distribution of surplus land among small farmers and landless labourers.

Some states, such as Haryana, Punjab, Maharashtra and UP, took the programme of consolidation of fragmented holdings quite seriously. A few states, with the blessing of the Central government, also encouraged experiments in cooperative farming. The guiding force in all land-related legislation during this period was equity and social justice.

Of these various reforms, measures to remove functionless intermediaries were quite successful. Results of tenancy reforms present a mixed picture. The landowners taking advantage of the provisions for 'self-cultivation' ejected a large number of small tenants. At the same time, a sizeable group of tenants, particularly the medium and large tenants tilling the land of absentee landowners, could secure tenancy rights and avail of lower rents. The same groups could acquire the land they were cultivating once the legislation on 'land to the tiller' came into force. The worst sufferers were sharecroppers and tenants-at-will. In most parts of the country, open tenancy was replaced by concealed tenancy; long-term lease contract to short-term leases; annual to seasonal lease; written to oral arrangements; and formal to informal contracts. Ceiling legislation was effective in hardly one or two states. Cooperative farming was a total failure.

There were two basic reasons for this less-than-expected success. With few exceptions, there was no mobilisation of beneficiaries to enable them to claim the rights provided in the legislation. In a system dominated by powerful vested interests, this was a major failing. Second, with the pre-occupation with equity, the aspect of productivity was not addressed in any meaningful way.

Measures described above were not without some favourable outcome. For example, we now have in the country a more or less uniform land tenure system, approximating to the *ryotwari* system, replacing a plethora of tenures. The reforms have, at least indirectly, contributed to the reduction in inequality in landholdings, as some evidence of the lower value of Gini coefficient suggests. Land reforms might have also helped in the emergence of a medium-size holding group at the expense of the large landholders. With all these favourable features, reforms have not helped in removing poverty and destitution among the small and marginal farmers. Nor do they seem to have contributed to the growth of non-farm employment.

Land Reforms, the Next Phase: A new phase of market-friendly land reforms as against the confiscatory type of land reforms—days for which are gone—is necessary. This, of course, does not preclude effective implementation of the existing ceiling laws. Even now, if the existing ceiling legislation is properly implemented, it would be possible to obtain at least one million acres of land.[4] However, one should not place high hopes to get additional land for redistribution in any substantial measure through this route. The next phase of land reforms should be based on the following major initiatives:

- Small and marginal farmers should be encouraged, and enabled, to expand their holdings by purchase of or by leasing-in land.

4. *Report of the Committee on State Agrarian Relations and the Unfinished Task in Land Reforms*, Department of Land Resources, Ministry of Rural Development, Government of India, New Delhi (2009).

- Supportive institutions of research, extension, credit and marketing should be geared to assist small farmers.
- The large farmers should be encouraged to sell or lease out land.
- They (large farmers) should be facilitated to start non-farm rural enterprises.

The legislation on ceiling on land could have helped in ensuring viable agricultural holdings by distributing surplus land to the marginal farmers. But this did not happen. Ceiling legislations were enacted in different states with the objective of sequestering land from large holdings and distributing the same to landless labourers or the marginal farmers. By all accounts, with the exception of one or two states, the effort was a failure. Area declared surplus was barely 6.6 million acres (about 2.8 million ha), of which 6.0 million acres was taken possession and 4.9 million acres was distributed among 5.5 million households, on an average each receiving less than an acre of land. There were loopholes in the declaration of ceiling land, in sequestering the surplus land and in distribution of the surplus land, and these are well known. But what is generally not appreciated is that ceiling legislation was intrinsically flawed, as surplus land was distributed in fragments of 1 or 2 acres to the landless workers. With such miniscule holdings, the sections who benefited from the reforms in terms of access to land did not have wherewithal to make productive use of land.

Land Markets to Help Small Farmers: In the present socio-economic milieu, land market could be used in favour of the small farmers to enable them to enlarge their holdings. Skepticism to use land markets as an instrument to help the small and marginal farmers is based on the fact that small farmers lost their lands to the bigger landlords, who controlled the credit and commodity markets as well. The situation has changed now. The 'Trinity' role of the large landholders is much weakened. But even today, the small farmers, on their own, will find it difficult to negotiate land purchase deals. Some agency of the state may purchase land at market price from large farmers and sell it to small farmers on reasonable terms. The state is already playing this role so far as land for industry and infrastructure is concerned. In fact, many state agencies are creating 'land banks' to attract industries in their respective states. Why can the same not be done to provide land to the small farmers to make their holdings viable?

For purchasing land from the market place or through some state agency, small farmers will need financial support. In the past, (i.e., in the initial phase of land reforms in our country), cooperative credit societies, especially the Land Development Banks (LDBs), assisted small farmers to buy land, and enabled tenant farmers to secure proprietorship rights. Such schemes exist even today, but they hardly figure in the portfolio of RFIs (rural financial institutions). Provisions for financing land purchases by the LDBs and refinancing of these advances by National Bank for Agriculture and Rural Development (NABARD) should be made more effective.

Unfreezing the Lease Market: In theory as well as in practice, lease transactions are helpful in more efficient use of land and labour resources. Yet, at present, leasing out of land by marginal as well as large farmers is illegal in many states, restricted in several others. As a result, the bulk of leasing arrangements are concealed. This leads to sub-optimal results, as the premium for the risk entailed in such arrangements has to be added. Objective of enabling small farmers to increase their operational area can be met to a large extent, if there is a free market for leasing land.

A major step forward in that direction will be if farmers with very small holdings are permitted to lease out their land to other marginal and small farmers on long-term basis, without losing their ownership right. Holdings with less than a hectare of land account for nearly 35 million hectares of land. Owners of these tiny parcels are not able to earn sufficient income to make both ends meet. Presumably, a part of this land is already leased out, overtly or in concealed manner, yet substantial part remains with the owners who are not in a position to earn enough income from the land and have to depend on farm and non-farm labour.

The large farmers can also release more land to lease out than what, with the prohibitive and restrictive laws, they are doing today. In order to ensure that unfreezing of the lease market is not used to defeat the purpose of ceiling on agricultural holdings, it may be stipulated that the operational holdings with leased-in land should be within the ceiling limits.

Three conditions have to be fulfilled if we have to reach the objective of assisting the small farmers in a 'free lease market': (i) proper record of rights; (ii) clear annunciation of rights and obligations of the landowner and tenant; and (iii) effective machinery for monitoring and adjudication at the ground level. Lease market will be effective only if those who are leasing out land can retain their ownership rights, and enough opportunities for non-farm employment are available to them.

For the latter to happen, large farmers should be encouraged to vacate (sell or lease out) the land in favour of small farmers and engage in post-harvest operations, in trade, agroprocessing and other rural industries. This group has resources, access to institutional support and capacity to bear risk, all of which are important to start an enterprise.

These initiatives will be in accordance with what is actually happening at the ground level. At the two ends of the spectrum, i.e., among the farmers with miniscule holdings and ones with large holdings, agriculture is not the main source of income. Of course, the sources of non-agricultural income differ in the two cases. It is wage income and income from livestock in one case, and interest, profits and rent in the other.

Encouragement of Non-farm Employment: Even with all these measures, a large number of the marginal farmers will not be able to subsist on land. It is important that in any strategy addressed to improve the lot of small and marginal farmers, non-farm employment should receive highest importance. One obvious avenue to increase non-farm employment is to strengthen the natural resource base of Indian farming. There is enough scope to use labour-intensive methods for strengthening land and water resources. Ingenuity lies in designing ways to make people, who benefit from these improvements, pay for the benefits. The MGNREGA provides excellent opportunity to offer gainful employment to marginal farmers along with landless workers, while strengthening the land and water resources in the rural areas. At the same time, scope for massive programmes of rural industrialisation should be recognised. With the participation of large farmers and technical and institutional support by relevant agencies at the taluka and district levels, a demand-driven programme of rural industrialisation should be mounted in all earnestness.

We can learn valuable lessons in this regard from the Chinese experience in the earlier phase of the New Economic Policy. During that phase, the break-up of the communes in small peasant holdings (the average size of these holdings was less than one-third of the average size of holdings in India) lead to a spurt in non-farm activities. The main reason for the growth of non-farm activities in China was that along with introduction of Household Responsibility System (HRS), severe price distortions in agricultural produce were also removed to a considerable extent. Both these developments provided the necessary incentive to boost agricultural productivity, which was already very high, especially in comparison to India. With higher production and better prices, the cash income of the farmers increased significantly, leading to an upsurge in their demand for non-farm goods and services.

There were other factors responsible for the phenomenal growth of the non-farm sector in China; the most important among these being a much higher investment in human resources, education and health, which preceded the institution of HRS, in programmes such as Spark Programme. Also, much more effective technological support was ensured to the small peasant holdings by linking technical institutions with farming. However, the main reason was the strong demand-induced linkages forged between agricultural and non-agricultural sectors.

In India, nothing of that sort happened. Income, particularly the cash income, of majority of the cultivators remained abysmally low. Naturally, they could not provide markets for non-agricultural goods and services. Only the rural rich could provide markets for non-farm sectors, and goods with high capital and high import components dominate their consumption pattern, as that of the richer sections of urban population. It is not surprising that such goods find an expanding market in the rural areas, while the rural arts and crafts languish. For survival of the latter, several other pre-conditions have to be fulfilled, e.g., skill development, better quality, reduced cost, institutional support, infrastructure development, etc., but the most important component in reviving rural non-farm activities would be an increase in the income of the large mass of small and marginal farmers. The change in agrarian structure is a pre-condition for this to happen.

A three-pronged strategy of stricter implementation of ceiling legislation, unfreezing lease market and operating land market in favour of the small farmers is consistent with the present liberal regime. This will also enable efficient agriculture and demand-induced rural industrialisation.

References

Ali, Ifzal, B.M. Desai, R. Radhakrishana and V.S. Vyas (1980). "India 2000: Agricultural Production Strategies and Rural Income Distribution", *Mimeo*. Ahmedabad: Indian Institute of Management.

Ministry of Agriculture (2012). *Agricultural Statistics at a Glance, 2012*. New Delhi: Government of India.

Sen, Abhijit and M.S. Bhatia (2004). "Cost of Cultivation and Farm Income", *State of Indian Farmers: A Millennium Study* (Vol.14). New Delhi: Academic Foundation.

Vyas, V.S. (2009). "Land Reforms: The Next Phase", in D. Narasimha Reddy (ed.), *Agrarian Reforms, Land Markets and Rural Poor*. New Delhi: Concept Publishing Company.

8

Food Security in India

*Can We Eliminate Hunger and Malnutrition in the Foreseeable Future?**

There is unanimity of opinion in our country, as in most other countries of the world now, that every person in a civilised society deserves to be food secure. A pledge to ensure food security (FS) has been repeatedly made at various policy fora and is incorporated in our development plans and policy documents. India is also a signatory to international convents to abolish hunger and malnutrition at the World Food Conference covenants by the Food and Agriculture Organization (FAO), and the Conference of Millennium Goals convened by the United Nations (UN). It has been endorsed as an important objective in our successive five-year plans.

The concept of FS as it is now understood universally goes beyond avoiding starvation. A universally accepted definition of FS suggests: "access to adequate food to all people at all times for an active and healthy life."

Due to difficulties in measuring FS, it is not possible to be precise on the degree of food insecurity that a household faces. However, food insecurity can be examined at three levels, *viz.*, hunger verging on starvation, calorie deficiency verging on hunger and malnutrition with or without calorie deficiency. There are obvious overlaps between these categories. Nonetheless, it is useful to accept these categories of food insecurity to distinguish the nature of deprivations faced by the households at these three levels and to arrive at appropriate remedial measures. In the following sections, I shall attempt the same. At the outset, I wish to make it clear that by using household, rather than

* R.S. Bhatt Memorial Lecture delivered at Bhavnagar University, 2005.

individual members of the household, as the reference unit, we are not taking into consideration intra-household distribution of food (between men and women, or adults and children)—a subject which is of great importance. In fact, it requires separate treatment.

Hunger

It is difficult to define or measure hunger. In India, the main source for finding out the number of hungry people comprises periodical surveys conducted by the National Sample Survey Organisation (NSSO). Their measurement of hunger is subjective, in the sense that what they record is the perception of respondents regarding their households getting 'two square meals' a day. On this count, there seems to be progressive reduction in the proportion of 'hungry' households among total households, both rural and urban, in every state for which time series data are available. Even with this laudable progress, the disturbing feature is that in 1999-2000, the latest year for which data are available, there were 1.6 per cent of rural and 0.4 per cent of urban households who did not get adequate food and had to suffer chronic hunger. In terms of percentage of the total number of the rural and urban households, these figures look insignificant; but when translated into actual numbers, it suggests that nearly 3.3 million households, comprising more than 20 million people, go to bed hungry every day. For a country which is aspiring for a growth rate of 8 per cent or more, feeding less than 2 per cent of its people who are chronically hungry should not be an insurmountable task. Other significant feature revealed by the NSSs is that some states such as, Assam, Bihar, Odisha and West Bengal (WB), continue to record higher proportions of hungry people as compared to the national average. And the proportion of vulnerable groups, on this criterion, is higher among the ST (scheduled tribe) and the SC (scheduled caste) households. If we have to fight this scourge, we have to concentrate on the eastern region of the country, especially socially and economically vulnerable groups therein.

The NSSs also reveal that hunger is more pronounced in certain months. The period of acute hunger varies from state to state but, normally, it is the post-sowing and pre-harvest months of July, August and September. Naturally, the worst sufferers are those who get only seasonal employment, i.e., agricultural wage earners and marginal farmers in rural areas of the arid and semi-arid regions. The plight of unskilled casual workers in urban areas is no better. The dry areas of Andhra Pradesh (AP), Gujarat, Madhya Pradesh (MP) and Rajasthan show severe incidence of seasonal hunger.

Some relief is offered by the Employment Guarantee Scheme (EGS) in the fight against seasonal hunger in the rural areas during the most difficult months. If properly targeted, EGS can provide gainful employment of 90-100 days to the vulnerable households during the slack period. We do not have any such programme for the urban areas, and this is a big lacuna.

Calorie Deprivation

In India, the poverty line is based on the quantum of calorie intake together with expenditure on other essential necessities accompanying the stipulated calorie intake. The base for calorie consumption for this purpose was estimated at 2,400 calories per person in the rural areas and 2,200 calories per person in the urban areas. Right from the inception, this norm was challenged, basically on two grounds. Some scholars (e.g., P.V. Sukhatme) do not consider a fixed calorie intake as a relevant intake at all, instead they suggest that body's adaptation mechanism determines the calorie requirement. They are not in favour of a fixed calorie norm for poverty estimation. Many others object to the relevance of the prevailing high norms. It has been suggested that, with the changing age structure, male-female composition, living standards, occupational diversification and availability of several facilities to minimise physical labour—all being reflected in changes in the consumption basket—the norms suggested are too high. This is also borne out by the fact that calorie consumption, even by the richest deciles in some of the major states, is less than the stipulated norms.

There is substantial force in this argument. The threshold calorie intake suggested for defining poverty seems to be on the higher side. However, one can easily agree that there is a 'minimum level' of calorie intake for ensuring 'healthy and productive life' and that consumption below that level signals food insecurity. FAO uses a cut-off of 1,810 calories for India that represents the lower range of food requirements. Based on NSS rounds, Vishwanathan and Meenakshi (2003) in a recent paper have shown that if the measure of 1,800 calories per person per day is used, there were in 1999-2000 eight states in the country where more than one-third of the population was consuming 1,800 calories or less per person per day. These were Tamil Nadu (TN), Kerala, Karnataka, Gujarat, Maharashtra, MP, AP and WB. It should be recognised that there has been some improvement in the situation as compared to 1983. Only four states—AP, Karnataka, MP and Maharashtra—recorded a higher calorie gap ratio as compared to their record in 1983.

Many of these states are not 'poor' states in the Indian context. It has prompted some scholars to challenge these norms as indicators of poverty. Their objection may be valid. However, the overall record in poverty alleviation in a state may hide calorie deficiency in some sections there. In any event, poverty and food insecurity are not one and the same thing. The fact that a large number of people in the country are not getting the minimum amount of energy necessary for good health is an incontrovertible fact, unless the NSSO estimations are wrong.

Assuming that the estimates of the number of people suffering from calorie deprivation are correct, such situation arose possibly due to two main reasons. Poverty is an obvious explanation. Or, the main sources of calories which the poor take recourse to have become too costly, and/or a higher expenditure has to be incurred on other necessities (e.g., health-related expenditure), thereby forcing people to cut down on the intake of food at the margin. There can, of course, be willing sacrifice of calories for looks, appearance, etc. Leaving aside the last motivation for low intake of calories, the other two more serious reasons clearly suggest policy and programmatic interventions. The relative prices of the foods that the poor consume for their sustenance have to be kept low, and the cost of availing of other necessities, particularly health services, has to be restrained. At present, the state is defaulting on both counts.

Nutritional Security

There is some evidence of progress towards eliminating hunger and, to an extent, even correcting calorie deprivation. There are no such hopeful signs as far as nutritional insecurity is concerned. In fact, several indicators of health and nutrition suggest deterioration of the situation. Indicators, such as body mass index, number of stunted and wasted children, maternal morbidity, and mortality, present a very discouraging picture. Thanks to the National Nutritional Monitoring Bureau and National Family Health Survey (NFHS), we have much better information on nutrition as compared to, say, hunger or calorie deprivation. These surveys unambiguously suggest that incidence of malnutrition is extremely serious. In 2000-01, about half of the children and one-third of adults were undernourished. What is more worrisome is the fact that, except for two states, Kerala and TN , there has not been any significant improvement in this regard. In some states such as MP and Odisha, the situation has worsened. Paucity of micronutrients, which is aptly described as 'hidden hunger', is equally glaring all across the country. In-depth reports on the plight of the poor in the regions, which record alarmingly high child mortality (death), point to the appallingly low nutritional status of children in these areas. Highest priority needs to be accorded to ensuring nutritional security for children. The nutritional status of adults is only slightly better. Chronic energy deficiency (CED) was as serious as child malnutrition, again, with the exception of Kerala and TN . MP, Maharashtra and WB showed the worst performance in this respect. In a large number of states, incidence of malnutrition among females is higher. According to the *India Development Report* (2004-05), brought out by the Indira Gandhi Institute of Development Research (Parikh and Radhakrishnan, 2005), medium income states such as Gujarat, Maharashtra and WB, do not fare much better than the 'less developed' or 'more advanced' ones such as Punjab and Kerala, or for that matter, the poorer states like Bihar, MP and the Northeastern states.

For ensuring nutritional security, special attention should be given to two groups: children in the age group 0.2, and pregnant and lactating mother. Improvement in the nutritional status of these groups will have a lasting and multiplier effect. Another group, which is becoming important, especially due to demographic transition, is that of the elderly persons who do not have any family support. Schemes such as old age pension legislated in some of the states have not gone beyond tokenism. The access of the elderly without family support to adequate nutritious food has to be ensured.

In short, the current scenario on the food and nutrition front suggests the following :

- Hunger, in terms of starvation, has largely been eliminated, although there is a disturbingly large extent of seasonal hunger, especially in dry areas.
- There has been progress in reducing calorie deficiency. However, a very large proportion of rural households subsist on below 1,800 calories per person per day even in the so-called progressive states.
- There has been no progress in ensuring nutritional security, barring in one or two states. The worst sufferers are young children, pregnant and lactating mothers, and elderly persons without any family support. If the present rate of progress in this area continues, India will not be able to reach the millennium goal of halving malnutrition.

In a country that has been aspiring for decades to achieve food and nutritional security, these are very disheartening facts.

If we have to redress this situation, review of the economic policies as well as the design and implementation of programmes to ensure FS is necessary. In the next section, we briefly touch upon the relevant economic policies. The following section highlights efficacy of the different programmes aimed at ensuring FS.

Economic Policies

Economic policies relevant in this context are those addressed to improving availability of food, ensuring stability in the supply of food and entitlement of households to food.

As far as availability of food is concerned, the last decade marked a reversal of the earlier trend, i.e., food production comfortably outpacing the growth in demand for food induced by increases in population and income. In recent years, income-induced growth in demand is slackening and the overall elasticity of demand is estimated to be between 0.2 and 0.3. However, population growth continues to be high at 1.9 per cent per year. Food production in recent years is creeping at 1.7 per cent per year. It is slower than the growth in population. Per capita foodgrain output is falling since the mid-1990s. The deceleration in the growth of production of foodgrains has been due to the complacency generated by the high level of production in the past. Two prime movers for the growth in productivity, namely investment in infrastructure, and generation and propagation of superior technologies, were neglected in the recent years. Complacency was partly induced by the belief that with the opening up of the economy, food surpluses available in the international markets could always be tapped.

So long as a large proportion of the workforce, currently accounting for nearly 57 per cent, depends on agriculture—and to a large extent on foodgrains production, and a sizable share of consumers budget goes for the purchase of food, it is imprudent to slacken our efforts to raise productivity in agriculture in general and foodgrains production in particular. Once this scenario changes, when non-agricultural sectors account for a bulk of employment and expenditure on food goes down to an insubstantial level, we can relax our policy of food self-sufficiency. Any premature withdrawal from this policy at this stage will jeopardise the FS of a large number of poor producers as well as a substantial section of poor consumers. This is not an occasion to spell out the strategy for imparting buoyancy to the agricultural sector. It is sufficient to indicate that the direction in which we should move is higher investment in land and water, along with strengthening the support systems of research, extension, credit and marketing. An equitable price policy has also a role to play. However, the present price policy, which has restored the adverse terms of trade for agriculture to a more equitable level, cannot be faulted.

Another important prerequisite at the policy level is ensuring a reasonable level of stability in the flow of food supply and also prices. Agricultural production being seasonal, some fluctuation in food availability and consequently in prices is inevitable and, in face, even desirable. However, as food is demanded every day and also accessed at frequent intervals, if not daily, by the poorer sections of consumers, excessive fluctuation in prices takes its toll on food consumption. More so as the employment opportunities for a large section of the people are also seasonal. In the situation of comfortable supply at the overall level, a properly functioning market can even out sharp fluctuations quickly and efficiently. The objective of our domestic market reforms is to remove imperfection in the markets and curb tendencies for monopolistic gains.

Procurement of major foodgrains at the MSP (minimum support price), coupled with an active buffer stock policy, also helps in assuaging large-scale deficits or surpluses in the availability of foodgrains. The situation can be further improved by a complementary trade policy. The government policies in the past were directed to soften the blow of fluctuations in the supply, with timely release or accelerated procurement as the situation warranted. Existence of a vast number of public distribution outlets (fair price shops) helped in the implementation of this strategy. In the absence of government interventions, fluctuations in prices would have been much sharper. This is one area where the government cannot abdicate its responsibilities.

The key consideration is the entitlement to food at the household level. For the bulk of the rural poor, who are threatened with food insecurity, entitlement is synonymous with their current income, mainly the wage income or the income from their paltry landholdings. The model of development practised in our country as well as in many other countries has led to growth of the jobless. This is also true of agricultural growth, where, with the current production pattern, employment elasticity is coming virtually to zero. The compound annual rate of growth in employment (principal + subsidiary) in agriculture during the period 1983-84 to 1993-94 was 1.39 per cent; it came down to 0.05 per cent during 1993-94 to 1999-2000. In this context, the EGS, if properly implemented, can prove a boon to the rural poor. Also, proper use and development of land and water resources can lead to diversification to more labour-intensive crops.

A major factor determining access to food, especially by poor households, is the relative prices of food. A cardinal principle of our food policy in the past few decades was the conviction that the real prices of food are kept low, while the farmers gain in income with enhancement in productivity. In the last few years, public support to enhancing productivity by investment in rural infrastructure and focusing attention to research and extension has been kept on the back-burner, and reliance seems to have been placed solely on the so-called 'incentive price'. The net result is that productivity has stagnated and real prices of foodgrains started creeping up. This policy is counterproductive. Like any other producer, the agricultural producer is concerned with his income, not with the prices *per se*.

A point which has to be made clear at this stage is the nature and justification for self-provisioning. In our anxiety to go for high value agriculture, the traditionally diversified farm economy is being disrupted. Fast disappearance of the crop-livestock nexus at the farm level is an example of blind faith in monoculture, favouring high value crops. So long as the access to inputs and output markets is biased against small farmers and insurance cover is not available to them, it will be a better strategy to encourage self-provisioning of nutritious food such as vegetables and fruits on small farms. I may mention that Thailand, another fast developing country like ours, is encouraging a policy of self-provisioning on small farms with a salutary impact on food and nutritional security.

Programme Interventions

There are three major programmes, which can make an important contribution to FS. These are: (i) the PDS (public distribution system) and its variant Antyodaya, (ii) Integrated Child Development Scheme (ICDS), and (iii) Mid-Day Meal (MDM) scheme. These are multi-objective programmes, but they can significantly contribute towards FS. A few words on each of these may be useful.

Among these, PDS, or its earlier versions, is the oldest programme. A large quantity of foodgrains and a few other necessities are distributed through fair price shops under this programme. In terms of the quantity of foodgrains handled and the number of outlets, it is one of the largest programmes of its kind in the world. Its effectiveness in reaching the poor has all along been questioned, mainly because of the lacunae in its implementation and leakages to non-merit consumers. These defects have been progressively corrected, even though much remains to be done. In a number of states, its scale and reach among the poor are progressively improving.

The real difficulty is due to the persistence of confusion regarding its objectives. Put simply, policymakers are not clear as to whether the objective is to influence the market prices through the supplies distributed through PDS, or to provide foodgrains to the targeted clientele at below market prices. Related to it is another question, one regarding the issue price, i.e., the price at which foodgrains are distributed to the poor. If the objective is to provide food to the poor as an indirect measure of income support, the issue prices should be substantially below the market prices. Pursuing this strategy is becoming more and more difficult as the MSPs, which have become synonymous with procurement prices, are progressively rising. The difficulties get compounded once the targeted distribution (i.e., targeted to the BPL [below poverty line] families) of foodgrains is abolished and foodgrains are made available to virtually every one through PDS. The net result will be food subsidies rising year after year, which is considered undesirable from the point of view of fiscal management.

The government seems to have taken the easier course. The issue prices are progressively rising, and the scheme has been opened to all types of clientele—those below the poverty line as well as those above. The paramount consideration is to reduce the subsidy burden. An approach consistent with the original objective of making food below the market price available to insecure households would suggest that the scheme should be confined to BPL households. This will automatically reduce the subsidy burden. And as the number of BPL households will, hopefully, continuously decline, the subsidy burden will come down progressively. The main argument against this approach is the difficulty in targeting. This is not the only programme for which a distinction is made between BPL and APL (above poverty line) households. We have to perfect the norms and procedures for targeting rather than throw away baby with the bathwater. I may mention here that the *Mid-term Appraisal of the Tenth Plan* suggests improvement in correlation between offtake from PDS and total number of the poor in the states.

A programme which can directly contribute to alleviation of the calorie deficiency is the Antyodaya programme. Started in December 2000, it was expected to identify 1.0 crore 'poorest of the poor' familes and make food available to them at highly concessional price, i.e., ₹2 per kg of wheat and ₹3 per kg of rice. The number of the poor to be covered has since been raised to 2.5 crore families, and the issue of foodgrains per family from 25 kg per month to 35 kg per month. If the programme is better targeted, it can certainly take care of the calorie deficiency for the worst affected sections.

Two other major programmes to ensure food security are the ICDS and the MDM programme. There is also the Annapurna programme to provide foodgrains to indigent senior citizens free of cost. This has yet to make its impact felt. ICDS is aimed at providing supplementary nutrition, along with health care, to young children and lactating mothers. It is a laudable objective, as it addresses the problem of malnutrition of those sections that need urgent attention. By focusing on children and young mothers, the programme ensures lasting benefits to the society. There is nothing wrong with the concept; the difficulties are more at the operational level, and are to be tackled with foresight and determination. The MDM programme is equally laudable. By providing nutritious food to the schoolgoing children of poor households, it encourages school attendance, apart from enhancing their nutrition levels. Whatever lacunae have been observed exist at the implementation level. An important development that is taking place in this programme in some states is PPP (public-private partnership). With the passing of the Right to Information (RTI) bill, an important step has been taken to ensure accountability of the programme implementers.

We have, thus, some powerful programme addressing the poor and the food insecure. Two vulnerable groups which are yet left out of the safety net are children in the 0-2 years age group and out-of-school youth. There is a need for well-focused nutritional interventions for these groups.

The ongoing programme, together with the policy reforms mentioned earlier can address the FS issues in an effective way, provided a major handicap, namely poor health and sanitary conditions, is addressed simultaneously.

Health and Environment

Over the years, we have gained in terms of life expectancy. The expectation of life at birth has doubled in the last 50 years. But, this has also given rise to higher incidence of morbidity. Apart from the malnutrition and lessened resistance to diseases, increasing pollution, crumbling sanitation facilities, deteriorating water quality and rampant adulteration of food items have added to the incidence of morbidity.

If the share of expenditure on health services in the total government expenditure, even in GDP (gross domestic product), for that matter is taken as an indicator, our record is worse than those of some of the other developing countries, particularly China. For example, we spend 5.3 per cent of the total government expenditure on health as against 11.0 per cent by China. Further, allocation of the public resources is biased against the rural areas. The private health providers, who have filled the vacuum are more expensive, though not necessarily more effective. As a result, the share of expenditure on health even among the poorer sections is rising without perceptible improvement in their health status. An inevitable consequence of higher expenditure on private health services by the poor is a decline in the share of expenditure on other necessities. (This, more than Engel's Law, explains the declining share of expenditure on food by the poorer households.) By all accounts, sanitary conditions in the rural as well as the urban areas are appalling. With totally inadequate health care and deteriorating environmental conditions, intake of nutritious food is no better than storing water in a sieve.

The Way Forward

We have made significant progress in eliminating hunger, although seasonal hunger is still rampant, and its incidence on some sections is very serious. We have not made much progress in filling in the calorie gap. The nutritional status in large parts of the country is probably deteriorating. If the objective of ensuring a healthy and productive life to all households is to be fulfilled, a time-bound programme to meet four critical requirements for FS have to be met: i.e., (i) adequate availability, (ii) reasonable stability in terms of quantity and price, (iii) purchasing power to access food, and (iv) desired nutritional intake. Let me summarise some important actions needed in these areas, based mainly on the previous discussion.

Availability

The first condition for ensuring FS is availability of adequate quantities of foodgrains to meet the requirement of the country's population. In the modern interconnected world, there is always possibility of importing foodgrains to supplement domestic production. This has prompted many analysts to suggest that we need not insist on food self-sufficiency. It need not be an article of faith. However, we have to continue with this policy as long as a large proportion of the agricultural producers, most of whom are resource-poor, are compelled to depend on food production for their livelihood, and a large part of consumers' expenditure—nearly 50 per cent of the total expenditure in the last two deciles—on food. Once these conditions change, i.e., we have, say, less than a quarter of agricultural producers depending on foodgrains production and a not too large amount of consumers' expenditure, say less than a quarter, being spent on purchase of foodgrains, we can review the policy on food self-sufficiency. These conditions will, hopefully, be met over a period of time. Until then, any heavy dependence on imports will expose the poor producers and poor consumers to risk, which they are not in a position to take. Our system is not resilient enough to accommodate all those who are likely to be displaced by heavy imports of foodgrains in other gainful activities, or even to facilitate their switching over to alternative crops on a scale warranted by such a shift in policy.

With concerted efforts, we have transformed a heavily import-dependent agricultural economy into one of food self-sufficiency, in fact one with exportable surpluses. It has been largely due to several policy and programmatic interventions. The more important among these being:

- concerted efforts in research and extension to evolve and popularise HYVs (high yielding varieties),
- investment in expansion of irrigation,
- assurance of a MSP and needed arrangements for procurement, and
- orienting the support institutions in credit and marketing to meet the needs of a dynamic agriculture.

All these measures continue to have the same relevance today. A significant change, which has taken place in the agrarian structure since the 1970s, is a larger proportion of the agricultural land being now farmed in small holdings, of less than 2 ha. The supportive institutions, both public and private, have to take account of the small farm character of our agriculture.

Another requirement for ensuring food availability in a large country like ours, with an underdeveloped rural infrastructure, is making sure that the domestic markets function efficiently, especially in the remote areas, and *vis-à-vis* small producers and consumers. The measures, which need to be encouraged in this regard, include:

- improving connectivity,
- developing efficient ways for price discovery,
- expediting the reform process in domestic markets,
- improving market infrastructure,
- ensuring an appropriate institutional arrangement to handle small lots in an efficient way.

Stability in Supplies

Food production being seasonal and the demand for food being more or less constant the year round, some degree of fluctuation in availability and in prices is inevitable. Apart from many other costs, the cost of storage over the seasons has to be reckoned with. Consumers also would accept some degree of fluctuation as inevitable. However, the poorer sections that buy their requirements on a day-to-day basis suffer the most due to the instability in supplies as well as in prices. In the years of crop failure, in the regions where shortfall in production takes place, there is always the danger of foodgrain hoarding by unscrupulous traders which aggravates the plight of the poor households. An important institution to protect the poor in such circumstances is 'grain banks', organised by a number of NGOs (non-governmental organisations) in different parts of the country. Realising the difficulties faced by consumers, especially in the 'lean seasons', certain measures seem imperative. These would include:

- a well-formed policy on buffer stocks and their release, i.e., an effective market intervention policy,
- a coordinated price and trade policy,
- use of PDS outlets to release adequate supplies in the lean seasons, and
- encouragement to organisation of 'grain banks' by the poor, on the lines suggested by the National Commission on Farmers.

Ensuring Access to Food

The most important condition for ensuring FS is entitling the household to avail of adequate nutritious food. For the bulk of food-insecure people, this means effective demand backed by the necessary purchasing power. For this reason, a high correlation of poverty and food insecurity can be observed. A large number of studies in this country have identified the agricultural labourers and marginal farmers in the rural areas and the casual workers in the urban areas as the most vulnerable groups. As most of the food-insecure households in the rural as well as the urban areas have to rely on wage-paid employment, provision of employment opportunities to these sections is the most important step. As far as marginal farmers are concerned, gainful non-farm employment is the right answer. However, there is a sub-set of these farmers who are potentially capable of enhancing the productivity of their small or 'marginal' holdings. It is important to remind ourselves that what we categorise as a marginal holding is the average size of holdings in most Southeast Asian countries as well as in China, with a much better record of agricultural productivity. In the past, some attempts were made to address the problems of these sections under Marginal Farmers and Landless Labour Development

Agencies (MFLLDA). Abolition of this programme proved to be a retrogressive step, as it led to neglect of the problems of this vast section of our rural population.

There is a residual section of the population who cannot avail of existing employment opportunities because of their physical handicaps. Old, infirm and physically challenged people cannot be left to their devices to procure food. Societal obligations should give precedence over all other considerations as far as FS to these sections is concerned.

Necessary measures to ensure access to food to the food insecure include:

- focusing on the proposed Employment Guarantee Programme (EGP) during the lean season in the selected districts,
- converging all employment-related programme in those districts which are not yet covered by EGP,
- reviving MFLLDA,
- starting Urban Employment Guarantee Programme with emphasis on skill formation and self-employment, and
- ensuring FS, as a matter of right to those who cannot do physical work.

Nutritional Security

There is no need to emphasise the appalling state of nutrition in our country. Judged by any indicator (body mass index, child mortality, maternal mortality or incidence of morbidity), India comes near the bottom in the list of comparable countries. In fact, on some indicators, we are worse off than some of the least developed countries. There have been no signs of any remarkable improvement in this respect in recent years. The irony of the situation is that most of the measures taken to improve the nutritional status do not require huge investment. The more important among the measures advocated by nutrition experts are:

- giving focused attention to the children in the 0-2 years age group, and pregnant and lactating mothers,
- identifying other vulnerable groups and administering food

supplements to these people through various government schemes,

- using PDS outlets for distribution of nutrition-rich food supplements,
- launching a kitchen garden movement in the rural areas and, wherever possible, in urban areas also, with distribution of seeds, planting material and advice on cultural practices for locally suitable fruits and vegetables,
- identifying nutrient-rich traditional crops and encouraging research on enhancing productivity and improving marketability of these crops, and
- Encouraging research on breeding nutrient-rich food crops e.g., high protein maize.

None of these measures will succeed without raising public awareness on the nutrition-related issues. In this task, as for other programmes for ensuring FS, civil society institutions will be more effective than the government machinery in mobilising people.

Neither dearth of resources nor lack of expertise can be cited as reasons for further delaying the task of ensuring a food secure India.

References

Parikh, Kirit and R. Radhakrishnan (ed.) (2005). *India Development Report, 2004-05*. New Delhi: Oxford University Press.

Vishwanathan, Brinda and J.V. Meenakshi (2003). "Calories Deprivation in Rural India, 1913-1944/2000", *Economic and Political Weekly* 38(4).

9

Reaching the Unreached

*To Make Poverty Alleviation Programmes More Effective**

Introduction

In this paper, I am trying to pose the question that despite good intensions backed by considerable resources and a variety of programmes, why are we not able to substantially reduce the number of the poor households in our country. I have pointed out the missing links in our approach to poverty alleviation. I should make it clear at the outset that my thinking is mainly based on the observations as a field worker in the villages of Gujarat and Rajasthan, coupled with experience as an observer of the policymaking processes at the centre and the state level. I am not competent to engage in *shashtrath* with the *pandits*, on the subtle theoretical grounds or on esoteric ideological issues.

We can readily agree that a large section of population in our country is not able to avail themselves of the minimum standard of living. It is, however, difficult to identify precisely the bundle of goods and services, which may be considered essential for achieving 'minimum standard of living'. It is even more difficult to identify from the macro angle individual households who have access to all the ingredients of what may be considered essential for the minimum standard of living. To bypass these difficulties, income of the household is used as a common denominator to identify the poor. Households earning or obtaining income below certain level are considered to be BPL (below poverty line) or the poor.

---

* 23rd I.P. Desai Memorial Lecture delivered at the Centre for Social Studies, Surat, 5 March 2013.

An influential group of economists and policmakers further assume that for alleviating poverty of this group, high growth in GNP (gross national product) is the necessary condition, and that the fruits of growth will 'trickle' down to the lower strata of the society and will enable them to reach over the poverty line. Assumptions underlining these propositions have been seriously questioned (Sachs, 2005). In any case, in our country rather satisfactory rate of growth of the economy during the past decade has not made the anticipated reduction in poverty. Official figures on poverty reduction bear it out.

Income Poverty

Despite current slackening of the pace of economic growth, Indian economy had a satisfactory record in this respect. The country registered a growth of over 7 per cent per year in the last decade. Unfortunately, the high rate of growth could not be translated into substantial reduction in poverty. According to the Planning Commission's estimates, population in poverty stood at 29.8 per cent (in 2009-10). Nearly a decade and half back (in 1993-94) using the same (i.e., the Tendulkar Committee) methodology, it was estimated at 45.3 per cent. In other words, poverty reduction in this high growth phase was barely 1.0 per cent per year. However, it is claimed by the Planning Commission that during the 11th Plan, poverty ratio was declining at the rate of 1.5 per cent percentage point every year and that the pace will be accelerated during the 12th Plan. This will not be easy as the rate of growth in the coming five years is not likely to be as high as in the previous decade. In this scenario, it is all the more important to correct the major lacunae in our approach to poverty reduction. I wish to dwell on this theme in this paper. Before that, let me say a few words on the limitations of the current estimates of poverty.

The estimates of poverty based on National Sample Surveys (NSSs) are grossly inadequate for the purpose of identifying the poor or to measure the extent of poverty at the macro level. In the first place, figures of consumption revealed in the NSS household surveys are equated to the income of the households. Even for approximating to consumption expenditure of the households, there are problems in deciding on the weight of different articles in the consumption basket and the prices attached to various items in different locations and in different years. Secondly, two-point comparison based on these figures does not identify the households who have 'exited' from poverty or the ones who have newly 'entered' as the poor. Nor can these figures tell us who are chronically poor and who are transiently poor. Finally, these figures do not differentiate between various categories of the poor, and therefore are not helpful in assessing the vulnerability of different households.

To circumvent some of these limitations, scholars have tried to estimate 'poverty gap', or have used simpler versions, e.g., categorising households who have less than or equal to three-fourth of the income which defines poverty line. The households in this category have been identified as chronically or severely poor (Asha Kapur Mehta *et al.*, 2003). In another version, popularised by the World Bank, the poor are categorised in two classes: those whose income is a dollar a day ($1.25 a day to be precise) and those whose income is $2 a day (both in terms of purchasing power parity). On the World Bank criteria also, the number of the poor in our country is huge: nearly 400 million on dollar-a-day basis and 841 million on two-dollar-a-day basis.

Poverty as Deprivation

It is now well recognised that poverty has many dimensions, and low income can define only some of these. Poverty can be understood as deprivations and lack of choice in various domains—social, economic and political. Hence, poverty alleviation measures have to be multi-faceted. It is only due to my own limitations, I am focusing on the economic dimension of such deprivation, i.e., inability to meet basic human needs of food, water, clothing, shelter, health care and education due to paucity of income or lack of capability to earn sufficient income. I will review a few major government programmes to enable the poor to meet these needs and comment on their efficacy.

We are looking into poverty-related issues in the context of a reasonably fast-growing economy. One can hypothesise that the poor are not in a position to take advantage of the growth-induced opportunities because of the handicaps they face; mainly because they lack income-generating assets and as a result remain at the periphery of growth process. These assets could be physical assets (e.g., land), stamina to do labour, skill to meet the market demand, and access to financial or social capital. Having such assets is the minimum condition for participating in the growth process; it is equally important to have an opportunity to take advantage of these assets in the market place, i.e., to convert these assets into capital. A large section of population whom we identify as poor do not have income-generating assets.

To compound their disadvantages, these asset-poor households are concentrated in backward regions, and most of them suffer from social discrimination. The NSSs as well as some scholars have identified major characteristics of the poor. For example, there are a few occupational categories such as landless labourers, rural artisans and marginal farmers who account for the bulk of the poor. Certain social classes, such as *dalits* and *adivasis*, account for a disproportionately large number of the poor households. Certain regions of the country, e.g., rainfed areas with low productivity and high degree of climatic risks, and tribal and hilly areas with depleting natural resources, coupled with communication and transport difficulties have more than their share of the poor households (Mahendra Dev, 2008; Thorat, 2010).

An important measure of relief from poverty for a household is the access to and use of the income-generating assets. Such access can be self-generated, inherited or bequeathed, including that through government programmes. In this paper, I am focusing on the government programmes, which may be regarded as direct income-generating programmes. I will also look into the programmes that enable the poor to acquire income-earning capabilities, among other benefits. I may mention that in this paper, I am concentrating on the rural poor.

At the outset, I wish to acknowledge that the poor are heterogeneous groups with varying capabilities and handicaps, and therefore requiring action at the disaggregated level. However, the macro policies and centrally designed schemes and programme, on which I am focusing, are important, although they may need local adaptation to be effective. If we ignore the importance of macro-level interventions we will, in essence, be opting for 'hand holding' operation for each poor household as every household, nay every individual, is unique.

Measure to Alleviate Poverty

As I have mentioned earlier, deprivation and the lack of choice characterise the poor, and paucity of income is a major, although not the only, constrain in overcoming various handicaps. In our country, direct approaches to increase the income of the rural poor comprised: (i) access to land, (ii) promotion of self-employment, and (iii) provision of wage-paid employment. Let me briefly review the policies and programmes addressed to reach these objectives.

Access to Land

An important measure undertaken in the past for alleviating poverty and aiming at far-reaching structural change in the rural society was the Land Reforms Programme, which aimed at giving access to the land and security of tenure, thereby raising agricultural production and income of the rural poor. The outcome, however, fell far short of the objectives. A few words on the measures of land reforms as they unfolded at the ground level will substantiate above observation.

Although land reform is a subject in the preview of constituent states of the union, due to a national consensus on the direction of land reforms, actual legislation followed more or less same content and sequence throughout the country. Practically in all states of the country, the reforms proceeded in following stages:

- abolition of functionless intermediaries (such as *zamindars* and *jagirdars*);
- protection of tenants' rights and regulation of rent;
- ceiling on landholdings and distribution of surplus land among small farmers and landless labourers; and
- legislation aimed at 'land to the tiller'.

The guiding principle in all land-related legislation during this period was equity and social justice.

Of these various reforms, measures to remove functionless intermediaries were quite successful. Results of tenancy reforms present a mixed picture. The landowners taking advantage of the provisions for 'self-cultivation' ejected a large number of small tenants. At the same time, a sizeable group of tenants, particularly the medium and large tenants tilling the land of absentee landowners, could secure tenancy rights and avail of lower rents. The same group could acquire the land they were cultivating once the legislation on 'land to the tiller' came into force. The worst sufferers were sharecroppers and tenants-at-will. In most parts of the country, open tenancy was replaced by concealed tenancy; long-term lease contract to short-term lease; annual to seasonal lease; written to oral arrangement; and formal to informal contract. Ceiling legislation was effective in hardly one or two states. Cooperative farming, ranging from joint management of individually-owned lands to the pooling of land in one farm, was a total failure (Vyas, 2007).

There were two basic reasons for this less than expected success. With few exceptions, there was no mobilisation of beneficiaries to enable them to claim the rights provided by legislation. In a system which was dominated by vested interests, this was a major failing. Second, with pre-occupation with equity, the aspect of productivity was not addressed in any meaningful way. Even the sections who benefited from reforms in terms of better access to land and more secure rights in land did not have adequate wherewithal to make a productive use.

Self-employment

Main source of self-employment in the rural areas is access to land. Over a period of time, the landholding size of the poor farmers is shrinking. Although landlessness has not increased appreciably, the number of marginal holdings are increasing. Today they account for 85 per cent of the cultivating households, and 40 per cent of the cultivated land. Even with better productivity, they are not in a position to make both ends meet.

With disenchantment from the redistributive land reforms, measures to provide self-employment to the rural youth in non-farm sector were adopted. The flagship programme in this area is the Swarnajayanti Gram Swarozgar Yojana (SGSY), which is a later version of Integrated Rural Development Programme (IRDP). The main emphasis in SGSY is on the formation of SHGs (self-help groups) with the initial stress on group saving, later to be linked with the banks so as to obtain adequate credit to start viable business enterprise. With the collective security of the group, the loan recovery was not supposed to be a major problem. The government further helped the groups by giving subsidy on the loans advanced to SHGs by the banks.

There are several studies on the effectiveness of these groups in alleviating the economic status of the members of SHGs. They suggest that success of the groups are region specific; in some states, especially in Andhra Pradesh (AP), they have done reasonably well, but in large parts of the country, they have not been able to achieve the desired results. Two facts stand out as the major cause of their less than satisfactory results. One, goods produced by the groups had only limited markets. Two, the banks were not keen to advance sufficient loans to the groups, hence they were not scalable. The groups had reasonable success where they were federated in the larger collectivity, i.e., in the federations of SHG (as in AP) or had strong government backing at various levels of the government (as in Kerala and AP).

Another important measure to help in establishing small enterprises, which is being emphasised in recent years, is universal access to credit through inclusive banking. If credit is interpreted as command over goods and services, this measure can enable the poor to have access to productive assets, which can be utilised for household enterprise. Inclusive growth has been set as an ideal since the beginning of planning in our country. However, it has been mentioned explicitly as an objective during the 11th Five Year Plan period. Inclusive banking is considered as an important instrument for achieving inclusive growth (Rangarajan Committee, 2008, Radhakrishna Committee...). Various measures have been taken to translate the policy of inclusive banking into a reality. These measures have definitely helped a large section of the people to avail of the banking services, more importantly the credit for own enterprises. Yet, as I will discuss later, there are large gaps on the supply side as well as on the demand side.

The self-employment programmes for the poor have not made any significant contribution to the alleviation of rural poverty. Lack of credit is only one of the hindrances to self-employment. The more important handicaps are lack of skills and weak market link. Wherever these handicaps were removed, a substantial number of the poor could engage in viable enterprises.

Wage-paid Employment

Until the advent of Mahatma Gandhi National Rural Employment Guarantee Act (MGNREGA), the main avenues for employment for the poor in the rural areas were agriculture labour and unskilled jobs in the non-farm sectors. The more serious problems in this regard are not that of open unemployment as that of the seasonal unemployment, disguised unemployment and unremunerative employment. MGNREGA is designed to address these problems. Employment for 100 days to all able-bodied persons at the minimum wages is assured. Wherever it is implemented properly, it also influences agricultural wages, making them rise in sympathy.

As in the case of other programmes, its success varies from region to region. In the more advanced regions, e.g., Punjab, the people do not demand work under this scheme, and in the backward regions such as Bihar and Jharkhand, organisational deficiencies do not permit all the deserving persons to avail of the employment guarantee. The record is slightly better in areas where the Panchayati Raj Institutions (PRIs) are made active partners in implementation of the programme, and where civil society groups perform the watchdog function, or where government takes the programme seriously.

The major criticism of the programme is that at best, it ensures unskilled work among the participants, with little hope of their acquiring necessary skills for opening up opportunities for sustained rise in incomes; also, except in few states, the assets created under the programme are not good enough to strengthen the production base in the region, and thus fail to remove the handicaps posed by infrastructure deficit. And, as with other government programmes, it is prone to corruption at all levels. With all these defects, it has helped the poor in the rural areas, especially those who are landless or have marginal holdings (Reddy...).

Government Programmes for Creating Capabilities

In last few years, any idea of major structural change in the rural areas is abandoned. Instead, programmes to enhance capabilities of the poor and enable them to have access to various services and facilities are being propagated. Some of these programmes are universal in their reach and in right mode; others are in terms of entitlements for BPL households. These programmes can be broadly divided into the following main categories:

- Food and nutrition security.
- Access to education and skill formation.
- Ensuring health.
- Subsidised housing.
- Support to special categories of the poor e.g., SCs (scheduled castes), STs (scheduled tribes), minorities, etc.

Despite the plethora of schemes, now operating for a number of years, a large section of the population suffer deprivation in terms of basic goods and services. We can look into two critical areas—one, eliminating hunger and ensuring nutrition, and two, education and skill formation—and see where a reasonable degree of success has been achieved and where the programmes have failed to reach the poor, especially those at the bottom rungs.

Eliminating Hunger and Malnutrition

In short, the current scenario on food and nutritional front suggest the following:

- Hunger in terms of starvation is largely eliminated, although there is disturbingly large extent of seasonal hunger, especially in dry areas.
- There is progress in eliminating calorie deficiency; yet a very large proportion of rural households subsist at below 1,800 calories per person per day, even in the so-called progressive states.

- There is no progress in ensuring nutritional security barring in one or two states, and the worst sufferers are young children, pregnant and lactating mothers, and elderly persons without any family support. Their plight is worst if the household belongs to the poor group (Vyas, 2007).

In a country that is aspiring for food and nutritional security for decades, these are very disheartening outcomes. If we have to redress this situation, review of economic policies as much as the design and implementation of programmes to ensure food security are necessary. There are three major programmes, which can make important contribution to food security. These are PDS (public distribution system) and its variant Antyodaya, Integrated Child Development Scheme (ICDS) and Mid-Day Meal (MDM) scheme. These are multi-objective programmes but they can significantly contribute towards food security. A few words on each of these may be useful.

Among these, PDS, or its earlier versions, is the oldest programme. A large quantity of foodgrains and few other necessities are distributed at subsidised rates through FPS (fair price shops) under this programme. In terms of quantity of grain handled as well as number of outlets, it is one of the largest programmes of its kind in the world. Its effectiveness in reaching the poor was always questioned mainly because of lacunae in implementation, and leakages to non-merit consumers. These defects have been progressively corrected, even though much remains to be done. In a number of states, its scale and reach among the poor is progressively improving (Mahendra Dev...).

A programme, which can directly contribute to the alleviation of calorie deficiency, is the Antyodaya programme. Started in December 2000, it was supposed to identify 1 crore poorest of the poor and make food available to them at a highly concessional price, i.e., ₹2 per kg for wheat and ₹3 per kg for rice. The number of the poor to be covered has since been raised to 2.5 crore families and the issue of grains per family from 25 kg per month to 35 kg per month. If the programme is better targeted, it can certainly take care of the calorie deficiency for the worst affected sections.

Two other major programmes to ensure food security are ICDS and MDM programme. There is also Annapurna programme to give free grains to indigent senior citizens, which has yet to make its impact felt. ICDS is aimed at providing supplementary nutrition along with health care to young children and lactating mothers. It is a laudable objective as it addresses the problem of malnutrition of the sections that have urgent need for it. By focusing on children and young mother, the programme ensure lasting benefits to the society. MDM programme is an equally laudable programme. By providing nutritious food to the schoolgoing children, it contributes to resolving food security problem of the households, and at the same time encourages schoolgoing habits among the children of poor households. An important development that is taking place in this programme in some states is the PPP (public-private partnership). There is nothing wrong with the concepts; the difficulties are, as in other poverty alleviation programmes, at the implementation level. I will refer to these in the latter part of the paper.

Education and Skill Formation

Education can be an important asset with the poor as it contributes to the quality of life, sense of well-being, general awareness and social networking. If combined with skill formation, it improves the prospects of remunerative employment. The cornerstone of educational edifice is elementary education. India's record in the area of primary education is a mixed one. After the start of the Sarva Shiksha Abhiyan (SSA), country has made tremendous strides in ensuring access to education, mainly the primary education. Nearly 99 per cent of rural habitations have access to primary education (*Mid-term Evaluation of the 11th Plan:* 125). Gross enrolment ratio is more than 100 per cent at the primary level. However, a large number of students are not able to continue after a year or two. Class one onwards, the enrolment progressively declines. It reaches 77.5 per cent after the upper primary level. Dropout rate is much higher for girls. Poor quality of education is the other major problem. Basic skills of reading, writing and arithmetic are at pathetically low level among the students, and there is no sign of improvement.

The other disturbing trend is growing privatisation and consequently higher cost of elementary education. Progressively larger numbers of schools are established in the private sector and larger proportion of students, even in the primary classes, are being enroled in privately run schools where the tuition fees are invariably high. This significantly adds to the cost of education. This tendency, which at the moment is largely seen in the urban areas but is spreading fast in the rural areas too, partly reflects the deteriorating quality of education in the government-run institutions. The net result is the growing inequality in access to education as well as in the quality of education. There is a risk that the impressive gains in terms of access to schooling that have been secured for all may become difficult to avail by the poor (Desai *et al.*, 2010).

Access to education is important in itself, but certain skills are needed for livelihood assurance. These skills are assets in themselves. With the disappearance of local arts and crafts, training in newer and more remunerative skills is necessary, which generally necessitates the knowledge of English and some computing skills. There are a whole variety of schemes and programmes managed by different ministries in the Government of India (GoI). States now have their own skill development programmes. A number of NGOs (non-governmental organisations) and private sector institutions are also engaged in this task. The results, till late were highly disappointing. According to 61st NSSO Round for the year 2004-05, among persons in the age group 15-29, about 1 per cent was receiving formal vocational training, about 2 per cent have received formal vocational training and another 8 per cent have received non-formal vocational training. There has not been any appreciable improvement in this regard, as the *Mid-term Appraisal of the 11th Plan* reveals.

The task is truly difficult because bulk of the labour force in the country is in the unorganised sector. The facilities for skill impartation are inadequate and the course curricula are outdated. Besides, there is no connection with the employability of the trained persons. As a result, even the inadequate training facilities remain underutilised. To correct the situation, a National Skill Development Mission is organised under chairmanship of the Prime Minister. The state governments are also advised to organise skill development missions. State Livelihood Missions are set up in a number of states, but the progress is tardy and the gaps in terms of number of training institutions, syllabi for training and employability of the trained persons are not bridged to any substantial extent. Thus, a veritable asset for the poor eludes them.

Making Poverty Alleviation Programmes More Effective

Despite all these programmes and schemes, we are not able to reach a large section of the poor. In order to redress the situation, we may have to concentrate on the following areas: appropriate designs of the programmes, reforming the delivery systems, building collective strength of the poor and creating an enabling environment. A few words in each of these factors are germane.

Designing Schemes to Suit the Poor

Most of the schemes aimed at poverty reduction are sponsored by the central government as central schemes or centrally aided schemes. The concerned ministries in the centre, and in some cases Planning Commission, frame them. When handed down to the states for implementation, invariably a set of guidelines is appended. The states generally interpret these guidelines as inviolable instructions and follow the same in the letter, though not necessarily in the spirit. Even the schemes framed at the state level give hardly any scope for adaptation at the field level. Introduction of the PRIs as institutions of decentralised governance has not helped the matters, barring in a few states, most notably in Kerala. In most of the other states, the functions devolved to the PRI level are still administered by the functionaries who consider themselves as representatives of their 'parent' departments rather than of PRIs, and consider the schemes proposed by the departments as sacrosanct.

Other common failing is the craze for uniformity. With the known diversity of natural and economic factors in different regions, 'one size fits all' approach cannot yield satisfactory outcome, and that is what is witnessed at the ground level. The characteristics of different groups of the underprivileged sections have to be taken into account before designing and implementing the programmes. To illustrate, any scheme for providing production credit to the poor for encouraging household enterprise should have a built-in component of consumption credit to finance their day-to-day needs during the gestation period of the project. Need for including consumption element was recognised way back in the 1970s by the Shivaraman Committee (Planning Commission....). But till date, consumption credit from the banks, and even from the cooperative credit societies, is an exception.

Similarly, while the poor get their income on daily or weekly basis, there is an insistence on purchasing bulk supply, generally for month, from the FPSs under PDS. Private sector has been more imaginative in this respect. For many of the consumer goods, quantities are made available in small packets at a price which is within the purchasing power of the poor. Also, duration of the schemes is not geared to the tasks envisaged. For example, schemes to encourage horticultural crops on smallholdings should give finance not for months but for 3-4 years. But term finance for the poor is practically non-existent.

Top-down and centralised approach to poverty alleviation programmes is not the only defect in our strategy for poverty alleviation. The major lacuna is the indifference to the needs and capacity of the poor. Low and unpredictable income and poor risk-taking capacity lead to demand-side constraints. These are aggravated with the cynicism generated by years of neglect and manifest opportunism of the ruling classes. The first task is to convince the poor that a particular scheme is of benefit to them and also that it is suited to their specific circumstances. It is important to generate a sense of ownership. The poor should be treated as partners and not as beneficiaries. The aim should be to make them self-reliant and not to perpetuate the dependency syndrome. Most of the poverty alleviation programmes, including a flagship programmes such as MGNREGA, fail on this score.

Other major failing in the design of our poverty alleviation programmes is the lack of convergence. The poor suffer from a variety of handicaps, which mutually reinforce each other. Lack of opportunities to earn income, poor education and skill level, bad health, and malnutrition all go hand in hand. Naturally, one scheme or a programme cannot correct all these limitations. Our past experience of Community Development Programme (CDP), which has been described by some critics, and not without reason, as a Christmas Tree Programme, suggests that this type of multipurpose programme soon becomes ineffective. What is needed is the coordination between various agencies administering different programmes. Presently, this is not happening. Every department administering a programme works in a silo and jealously guards its territory. Wherever the government, NGOs or the private sector makes a coordinated approach, each agency supplementing the efforts of the other, results are quite heartening. Thus, if a credit institution advances credit to the landless, a skill imparting programme is instituted by some institution for the young ones from the same households for teaching requisite skills, and a marketing agency is identified to market products of the household enterprise, the results achieved would be most satisfactory. There are examples of such coordinated efforts in which different agencies have participated and yielded satisfactory results, but these are exceptions.

Reforming the Delivery Systems

We have several pro-poor programmes, which look quite attractive on books. However, at the ground level, their implementation leaves much to be desired. It can be readily agreed that administering poverty alleviation schemes for a vast number of people, often in difficult terrains, is not an easy job. In resolving the problems of number and distance, technology can play a significant role as exemplified in a number of developing countries in credit disbursal to the poor (e.g., Bangladesh and Kenya), and in a few areas in our country. Access to appropriate technology can make a huge difference to the quality of life of the poor. As C.K. Prahalad (2005) has noted in his seminal book, *The Fortune at the Bottom of the Pyramid*: "Technology can provide the tools for the poor and the disadvantaged to be connected seamlessly with the rest of the world in a mutually beneficial and non-exploitative way."

The experience has shown that if the technology is appropriate, the poor do not hesitate to adopt it speedily. The spread of the mobile phone is a telling example. Mobile phone technology has opened new opportunities in our country to reach the unreached. We can make effective use of mobile phones, which are no more an elitist symbol, to deliver a number of services to the poor. Such examples can be multiplied.

Similar innovations have been tried at the organisational level in our country and in others. Banks have instituted banking correspondents who can substitute brick and mortar bank branches; local youth can take on the function of imparting elementary education; health services can be organised in different tiers from simple treatment to complex operations. If we are serious about reaching the poor, we should explore all possibilities of using appropriate technology and organisational change to ensure effective delivery.

Policies for strengthening delivery system have to grapple with the main problem of higher transaction costs to deal with the poor households, perceived higher risk in dealing with them, and limited capacity of the poor in absorbing high value inputs and credit. These three factors are advanced to explain ineffectiveness of the delivery systems *vis-à-vis* the poor. All these, as I will argue below, suggest the need for collective organisation of the recipients and certain initiatives at the government level. Another seemingly insurmountable difficulty is the urban bias of the government functionaries. However, the record of other implementing agencies is not much different. The functionaries have to be made accountable for the deficiencies in implementation. Right to Information (RTI) is an important step in that direction.

A paradigm shift is needed in management of the government-sponsored programmes. As Khandwala (2010) has argued, "a new public management system has to be introduced which treats the citizens as customers rather than beneficiaries and puts emphasis on outcome rather than allocation." Designing of autonomous agencies for programme implementation (e.g., Society for Elimination of Rural Poverty in Andhra Pradesh), professionalising officialdom, judicious use of PPP, devolution of the functions to PRIs to the people's representatives, and giving them the power of monitoring and supervision (as in Rajasthan in case of MGNREGA) are the steps to strengthen the delivery systems.

An important consideration while dealing the poor is that they have multiple handicaps. This as I have mentioned above needs convergence of several schemes and programmes at the delivery level. The agencies should be created to serve the poor. The delivery systems addressed to the poor should learn to live with *inter se* relationships among large number of institutions. In a culture where every institution is zealous in protecting its turf, it is not easy to have such coordination.

To ensure service delivery to the 'last man' and to avoid leakages and corruption, a new initiative, i.e., Direct Cash Transfer is proposed. The success of this initiative will depend on how soon the Unique Identity programme under Aadhaar is spread in the country, and how effectively the banking outlets are spread in remote areas. On both counts, a consdiderable amont of ground is yet to be covered. As per Reserve Bank of India (RBI) data, the number of bank branches in the country is around 40,000. To these may be added the business correspondents numbering approximately 1,16,000. These numbers have to be compared to nearly 6,00,000 villages in the country. It is clear that a large number of villages do not have banking facilities. Even with universal coverage under Aadhaar and banking facilities, not all the subsidies can be transferred to the beneficiaries through direct cash transfers. For example, food distributed through PDS has not only the subsidy element, but also meant to be, or could be, a step in the direction of ensuring food and nutrition security.

Building Collective Strength of the Poor

One of the common problems of the poor is that as individuals they have no identity, and no bargaining power. In the market place, they are always losers, whether it is the labour market or market for goods and services. Besides, there are activities, which can be profitably organised only if scale is imparted to them. These handicaps can be overcome with some form of collective organisation.

We have tried with different forms of organisations for collective action, from SHGs, to cooperatives, to producers companies. There are also examples of trade unions of agricultural workers. Not many of these organisations have succeeded for a length of time. But there are examples of successful cooperatives particularly in dairy and sugar sectors. Newer forms of aggregation for availing of inputs and marketing of produce, such as producers' companies, also have better record. For other types of successful collectivities, one can cite examples of several initiatives in AP (Velgu), Gujarat (SEWA) and Kerala (Kudumbashree), as well as of SHG federations in different parts of the country.

Such collective action is particularly important in productive activities, e.g., in production and marketing of artisans' and small farmers' products. There are certain features of successful group efforts, which need to be emphasised. The basic units of the successful collective entities are small homogeneous groups of members who constitute the primary unit; there is a dedicated 'agency' to initiate and support them for a length of time; there are distinct gains in productivity and/or realisation of higher value for their products; there is sufficient stress on capacity building. I will like to emphasise that in present circumstances, homogeneous groups of small producers, with joint efforts to cater multiple needs of their enterprises, can not only provide advantages of scale to their efforts, but also provide effective foundation for an equitable rural structure.

Integrating various functions such as input supply, extension and quality control, and more importantly, the marketing and processing with larger organisations in a vertical manner is another possible route. Even such arrangements will be more effective if producers' group rather than individual producer is a contracting party. We have now sufficient experience of working with different models of vertical linkages, and should be able to adapt them to the given circumstances.

Creating an Enabling Environment

If despite huge investment in the social sector and a plethora of schemes and programmes our record in poverty alleviation is unsatisfactory, it could be due to the absence of adequate physical infrastructure and conducive environment to conceive and implement pro-poor programmes. The absence of appropriate institutional safeguards reflects in hegemony of the rich and the powerful, and insensitive government systems and procedures. Gaps in physical infrastructure exacerbate these lacunae. As a result, one finds at the ground-level local monopolies, wasteful and insensitive implementing agencies, and inadequate access to markets for the poor.

All this is changing, although not at a speed one would have desired. For example, physical infrastructure, especially connectivity, is fast developing. (Importance of connectivity cannot be overemphasised as it can help to a great extent in breaking the institutions and arrangements that perpetuate local level exploitation.) It is evident from the fact that the districts identified as the Naxalite-affected and are among the poorest districts of the country are also, generally, most inaccessible districts. To create a road network in these districts has emerged as one of the most important programmes for their development. This would help in mobility and information sharing which are necessary, though not sufficient, conditions to convert the assets of the poor into capital and then into income streams. Significant progress has also been made in the regard to connectivity. But much remains to be done. On other two elements of local environment, namely hegemony of the rich and the powerful and insensitive and unimaginative bureaucracy, there is no perceptible change.

There are legal and institutional hurdles, which are more restrictive than infrastructure or administrative deficit for creating an enabling environment. A positive step to overcome institutional hurdles is entitlements for various services in a right mode. This strengthens the hands of the poor. It gives them access to goods and services without necessarily owning these. Other institutional and legal measures, such as RTI, have proved to be important tools to ensure transparency and accountability; PRIs have given opportunity to the poor to participate in the governance process; technology has made spread of information faster and easily available; physical connectivity is fast improving. A moot question is why all these changes are not manifesting in rapid decline in poverty. There are certain operational lacunae, particular at the design level and in the delivery systems to which I had referred earlier. The more abiding factor is the all-pervasive corruption.

It can be traced to the quality and character of our elected representatives, self-serving bureaucracy and amoral entrepreneurs.

There are exceptions in all these classes. There are politicians who are genuinely working for the downtrodden; they are honest and efficient state functionaries at all levels; there are business people who shun dishonest means. But they do not define the character of the groups they represent; they are exceptions. It will be wrong to single out any one of these groups as fountainhead of corruption, because corruption has become an acceptable norm of social behaviour. In this environment, the tasks of poverty alleviation and 'reaching the last man' get relegated to background. Corruption in various forms and types vitiates the intended objective of the legislation; and allows the powerful and well-connected to pre-empt all that is due for the poor and marginalised sections.

To leave one-third of the population behind in our quest for higher growth cannot be justified by any cannon of ethics. It is also bad economics, as sustainable growth, even in terms of GDP (gross domestic product), will remain elusive with such high burden of marginalised households. It is possible for us to make a marked improvement in our efforts to eradicate poverty if, first and foremost, an environment is created where a set of values are shared, mutual obligations are respected, and commitment to given tasks is considered sacrosanct. In such environment, it will be easy to correct some of the lacunae in the poverty alleviation programmes that I have highlighted.

References

Desai, Sonalde B., Amresh Dubey, Brijlal Joshi, Mitali Sen, Abusalath Shariff and Reeva Venuraman (2010). *Human Development in India.* New Delhi: Oxford University Press.

Mahendra Dev, S. (2013). "Food Security in India", *South Asian Journal*, Oct-Dec.

Government of India (1978). *Expert Committee on Consumption Credit* (Chairman: B. Shivaraman). Ministry of Finance and Planning Commission: New Delhi.

————. (2008). *Report of the Committee on Financial Inclusions* (Chairman: C. Rangarajan). New Delhi.

————. (2009). *Report of the Expert Group to Review the Methodology for Estimation of Poverty* (Chairman: Suresh D. Tendulkar). New Delhi: Planning Commission.

Khandwala Pradeep N. (2010). *Transforming Government Through New Public Management.* Ahmedabad: Ahmedabad Management Association.

Mehta, Asha Kapur, Sourabh Ghosh, Deepa Chatterjee and Nikhila Menon (2003). *Chronic Poverty in India.* New Delhi: Indian Institute of Public Administration.

Prahlad C.K. (2005). *The Fortune At the Bottom of the Pyramid.* Pearson Education (Singapore) Indian Branch, Delhi.

Narasimha Reddy D. (2011). *NREGS and Indian Agriculture: Opportunities and Challenges.* New Delhi: Institute for Human Development.

Sachs, Jeffrey, (2005). *End of Poverty: How We Can Make It Happen in Our Lifetime.* U.K.: Penguin Books.

Thorat, Sukhdeo and Katherine Sed Newman (2010). *Blocked By Caste: Economic Discrimination in Modern India.* New Delhi: Oxford University.

Vyas, V.S. (2000). "Ensuring Food Security: The State, Market and Civil Society", *Economic and Political Weekly* 35(50).

————. (2007). "Marginalised Sections of Indian Agriculture: the Forgotten Millions", *Indian Journal of Labour Economics* 50(1).

10

Weakening Roots of Democracy and the Role of Civil Society*

The widely accepted definition of democracy is that it is "a government of the people, for the people and by the people." It is almost impossible to run a system of governance in the true spirit of this, rather exacting, definition in the present circumstances. A government could be 'by the people' and 'for the people,' but a government 'of the people' is possible only in a society where a face-to-face democracy could exist. With increasing complexities in social relations and institutions in our society, it is becoming well-nigh impossible to have governance 'by the people,' and for that matter even by people's representatives. It is now difficult for the people's representatives to control the institutions of the government; even giving direction to these institutions is becoming difficult, if not impossible. In this context, there is a need for redefining the role of common citizens in a democracy, keeping in view the present realities and complications in institutions, programmes and functions.

In this paper, I will briefly touch upon the issues which could in my view make people's participation decisive in the modern state. In the first part, I will discuss the reasons why India opted for a democratic form of government and how distortions have set in our model of Democracy. In the second part, I shall draw your attention to the conditions essential for a genuine democracy. In the third and last part, I shall present my views on the role of civil society institutions in strengthening democracy.

---

* Mohan Singh Mehta Memorial Lecture delivered at Seva Mandir, Udaipur, 2003.

I

Even before Independence, it was clear that the system of governance in free India would be a democratic system, and that there would be no place for an authoritarian form of government. Now that we have become accustomed to this system over the last 50 years or more, we do not find it extraordinary, but the fact remains that it was a revolutionary idea at that time. Most of the countries getting independence around the time India achieved freedom failed to establish democracy. Even where democracy was initially adopted, the democratic systems were soon aborted. Several Asian, African and Latin American countries are examples of this phenomenon. In India, not only was democracy established but the democratic system—in its narrow definition, i.e., universal franchise, right to form political parties and timely elections—has remained in place since Independence.

There is a need to reflect as to why our experience is different from that of most other countries getting independence in the 1940s and 1950s. The main reason, in my view, is our traditions of pluralism and tolerance. Our culture does not give a unique and singular position to a person or on idea. Even our gods and goddesses number 33 crore. The greatness of different gods varies in different contexts. Different communities co-exist here and the dividing lines between them are blurred; there are no watertight compartments on the cultural plane. These characteristics are not confined to Hindu society only; the same traits of plurality and diversity can be seen in all religions that have got a foothold in this land. Indian society is not monolithic. And, this augurs well for democracy. Similarly, tolerance is considered a moral value in our society. Mao's saying "Let a hundred flowers bloom," which unfortunately could be realised only for a brief period in China, is a part of the Indian lifestyle. Even fundamentally divergent ideologies are expected to be tolerant of each other. Every 'ism' has a counter 'ism' and they are expected to co-exist. These initial conditions are favourable for democracy. If pluralism gives freedom of choice to people, tolerance can help in creating consensus on major issues.

Although these cultural traditions proved helpful in establishing democracy, they were not sufficient to ensure its continuation. For this to happen, a political base was needed. Fortunately, the process of the freedon struggle and the character of its leadership created the political base that was essential for establishment and continuation of democracy. Unlike in many other countries, the freedom struggle in India was not a movement of a handful of the elite. A huge mass of people participated in it, and its pervasive coverage was evident from time to time. Since a large number of people participated in the freedom movement, they could not be ignored after the attainment of Independence. It had to be ensured that there was people's participation in the governance after Independence.

The leadership of the freedom struggle, barring a few exceptions, had full faith in democracy, i.e., in Parliamentary Democracy. For example, special privileges to *rajas* and *maharajas* accorded in the beginning were soon withdrawn and they too were considered at par with common citizens. The leaders of the freedom struggle differed on several issues, e.g., the economic system to be adopted after Independence, but they were unanimous in supporting a democratic system of governance.

Despite these favourable conditions, the roots of democracy could not penetrate deep. We cannot ignore the fact that at present, democracy in our country has been reduced to a mere formality. No doubt, every adult citizen has the right to vote; elections are normally held in time; several parties and groups are in existence; the parliament and state assemblies meet regularly. But the sheet anchor of democracy—a government by the people and for the people—has been reduced to a mere slogan. Sadly, democracy, in the true sense of the term, has not taken deep roots.

Even if we leave aside the wider connotation of democracy, the main features that make it different from other systems of governance are under severe threat. One of these features is rule of law, and the other is civil liberties. Every citizen should be assured these two essential features of democracy. Judged on these criteria, we cannot call our democracy a successful one. Rule of law is not accorded primacy as evidenced by discrimination between various groups and individuals. Some people get more favourable treatment than others. Some are more equal than others. Similarly, violation of human rights, under one pretext or another, has become a common occurrence. Why does this happen?

Certain reasons for the erosion of democratic norms are common all over the world, but there are some other reasons for which we alone are responsible. All over the world, functioning of several government institutions is not only beyond the reach of the common people, but also incomprehensible to them. This is not necessarily due to absence of information or lack of education. Even in countries where the literacy rate is nearly 100 per cent and people do not have problems in getting information, certain units of government are beyond the control of democratic institutions. For example, the central bank of every country has become more or less an autonomous institution. There are institutions other that the central bank, particularly those concerned with internal and external security, which are slipping out of the control of parliaments and assemblies. The number of such institutions and the scope of their activities are increasing day by day.

One of the reasons for the erosion of democracy in India is the tendency to ignore the legislative branch by the executive wing. A ruling party feels relieved when the session of parliament and/or assembly is over. Today's politics is gradually becoming the politics of escaping the control of parliament and assemblies by the government of the day. We can call it "politics of evasion." Sometimes, one feels that the executive branch merely tolerates the legislative institutions as a necessary evil.

The defect does not lie solely with the executive wing and with the government in power. The way in which business is conducted in parliament and the assemblies—which now can be seen by every one on television—gives the impression that the members of these bodies are using these fora for their personal interests, or on behalf of some vested interests. At times, one suspects a hidden agenda even when the members seek information and ask questions in these august bodies.

The situation is becoming more complicated because of two interrelated reasons. First, the gap between the common electorate and their representatives is widening day by day, although it should have actually been bridged by now in view of the spread of education and rapid development in IT (information technology), transportation and communication services. The number of people's representatives who in their lifestyle, thinking and functioning truly represent the common people is fast disappearing. People's representatives are now getting identified by Mont Blanc pens, costly watches, designer suits, Italian shoes and the most advanced mobile handsets. The Khadi-Kurta-Chapal wearing leaders, hanging a bag on their shoulder and participating in the joys and sorrows of people, have become relics of the past.

Such degradation has set in not only among people's representatives, but the character of the society to which they belong is also changing. In the society, there is a rat race for cornering more facilities and resources than what one deserves, and our representatives owe their allegiance to one or another's vested interest in the society according to their convenience.

All these shortcomings are aggravated by rampant corruption. It starts with a situation where the mass base of persons seeking election is weak. Such representatives badly need money for wooing the electorate and to sustain the loyalty of their constituents after elections. The monetary value of votes is increasing because of competition among such "people's representatives" belonging to different and competing political groups. In the same ratio, the money needed to win elections and hold on to office is increasing. The cancer of corruption that starts with election gradually engulfs the entire society. I am not saying that the election process and the lifestyle and functioning of people's representatives are solely responsible for corruption. There are other reasons also. However, when we are talking about strengthening the roots of democracy, we cannot ignore one of the most important sources of corruption which is destroying these roots.

Before moving forward, I want to make two things clear. Whatever I have said about the character of people's representatives and the legislative and executive institutions is, in a sense, oversimplification. In a vast and diverse country like ours, genuine representatives of people and democratically functioning institutions do exist, even if they are exceptions. Second, if a sense of desperation is reflected in my statements so far, I must correct it. Despite several disabling conditions, the strength inherent in our democratic institutions can still be made overt and effective. In the remaining part of the lecture, I would like to lay emphasis on those conditions which are essential for strengthening the roots of democracy, and which, I think, are achievable.

II

In this part, I shall be expressing my views on the pre-conditions for a genuine democracy in aphorisms. I consider the following conditions essential for the survival of a genuine democracy.

- For those institutions where direct control of the electorate is not possible, explicit criteria for accountability should be established, and maximum transparency in the functioning of such institutions should be ensured. Making various programmes and activities opaque with excuses like 'in the interest of the security of the country' is not very convincing. In the present era of spy satellites, remote sensing and other scientific techniques, it is difficult to hide anything. There should be a system of social audit and performance evaluation conducted by experts, and the results of such investigations should be easily accessible.
- Democracy cannot be confined to parliaments and assemblies. Democratic functioning should inform other institutions of society as well, particularly the judiciary and the press. These institutions should not be oversensitive. They should allow scrutiny of their activities. Allowing an institution to function without transparency and accountability even as an exception is to prompt other institutions to follow the same practice. The criteria for transparency and accountability for different institutions will, naturally, vary.
- People's faith in democracy could be sustained only when they are assured that all are equal before the law. Today there is a feeling among some sections, especially among the minorities, that their interests and rights are not protected. If majority of the community acts in a fanatical and oppressive manner, it is

the duty of the government of the day to ensure civil rights of every citizen. Strong government should not be equated with dictatorship. It implies that the rulers have a strong political will and the capacity to act impartially. Those who value democracy are expected to support a government that is strict but fair.

- Democracy can succeed in a big country like India only when all the institutions of the state at every level have well-defined rights and responsibilities. Only when the central government, the state government, the district administration and the village *panchayats* become aware of their rights and duties, and function accordingly, the people of this country would consider the institutions of state at different levels as their own institutions.
- In a multi-party democracy, political parties are the pillars of the state. Internal democracy, transparency and accountability are equally important. If political parties in their internal functioning are run at the whims, fancies and biases of the so-called 'supremo' or 'high command,' one cannot expect that they will change their character after assuming power and run the government on democratic lines. Democracy is as important in the internal functioning of political parties as in the functioning of parliaments and assemblies.
- Consensus within a country on major issues is necessary for strengthening the roots of democracy. When there are fundamental differences between large groups on key issues of state and society, it becomes difficult to run the government on democratic lines. One of the pre-requisites for evolving a consensus, especially on economic issues, in a developing economy is economic growth, which enables a large number of people to participate in and benefit from the development process. I would like to emphasise that economic development is a minimum, but not a sufficient, condition for a functioning democracy. In a climate of economic stagnation, one cannot expect that a consensus on major issues could be evolved,

especially in a poor country. The tension caused by economic stagnation will be a constant threat to democracy.

- Tolerance is the biggest requirement for sustaining democracy. It has to be recognised that opposition does not mean enmity. Fortunately, as I mentioned earlier, tolerance has been recognised as a value in Indian culture. Inculcating this value in citizens' life is possible through education. I would not limit education to mere schooling and college degrees. Tolerance has to be given a place of pride in every aspect of our social and political life.
- In the mutually dependent world of today, establishment and protection of democracy in a country will be difficult without democratising world-level institutions. If we agree with this proposition, then it becomes our duty to make efforts to bring about answerability and transparency in international institutions, and strive for a 'level playing field.'

At the end of this part, I would like to stress that preservation of democracy depends on two basic conditions. First, only an alert and empowered citizenry can protect democracy. A society in which every citizen is aware of his or her rights and duties, where all the people get equal opportunities for playing their role, and where one can get institutional support for one's development without any discrimination, is a must. Second, the foundation of democracy is a set of values that are not simply specific institutional arrangements, although the importance of an appropriate institutional structure cannot be denied.

III

If the above preconditions are essential for strengthening the roots of democracy in India, it would be relevant to consider the responsibilities of institutions of civil society, particularly voluntary agencies, i.e., NGOs (non-governmental organisations). These days, there is not dearth of voluntary agencies in our country. In view of their large numbers and the wide scope of their activities, it has become necessary to be clear about their responsibilities towards the community they represent, for that matter, towards society in general. It is also important to understand their relationship with other institutions, especially Panchayati Raj Institutions (PRIs). Voluntary institutions are now emerging as the Third Sector along with the state and the market. Correspondingly, their importance and responsibilities have also increased.

The pace of development of voluntary institutions varies and that too in varying modes. They also have different working styles depending on the objectives they wish to achieve and the groups they are working with. Uniformity in the organisation and working of these institutions is neither possible nor desirable. However, despite understandable variability and differences in their working styles, commitment to the values of transparency and accountability is expected from all NGOs as from other institutions of our society. This is generally acceptable to the NGO community. And, it is a very good sign.

Apart from adhering to democratic values, such institutions are expected to perform certain specific roles which I shall discuss now. Voluntary agencies should be ready to take up three kinds of responsibilities for strengthening the roots of democracy. These responsibilities are: advocacy, protest and initiative.

Let us talk about 'advocacy' first. Despite laying full stress on universal representation, it is clear that in a democracy such as ours, certain sections of the society are marginalised and are not adequately represented in the institutions that take vital decisions impacting on socio-economic development, although such decisions affect their well-being in a profound way. Voluntary organisations are not expected to work like political parties for upholding the interests of their constituents. But, it is essential that pressure is exerted on all those who are part of the decision-making process in the interest of such neglected sections. The decisions that have been taken or have not been taken, but should have been taken at various levels, should be evaluated in terms of their impact on the underprivileged sections. The work of advocacy is not confined to protecting interests of the deprived sections, nor in fact it is possible for voluntary organisations to take up the advocacy role on all aspects touching the lives of the deprived classes. These institutions have also certain limitations in the scope of their activities. On the other hand, advocacy for issues impinging on the society as a whole, such as human rights, is also essential. The institutions may have to play the role of advocates on specific issues in the given context, e.g., issues such as environment, employment, education and health, which may be important for specific regions or groups.

The advocacy function can be conducted effectively only when the concerned institutions have complete information, and have reasoned views on the issues and approaches. Effective advocacy is not possible without fully understanding the issues and their implication in the given societal context. Since the decision-making bodies command power and resources, NGOs who plead on behalf of the disadvantaged groups need to strengthen themselves by forming alliances, and networking with organisations that work in the same or similar areas.

While formulating the strategy for advocacy, it is necessary to understand that in a society like ours, which is, relatively, an open society, we need to be active at various levels. It is essential to organise the neglected classes themselves for making their voice effective. At the same time, the opinion makers in the society, e.g., academics, journalists, subject matter specialists, etc., would have to be convinced. Simultaneously, exerting pressure at the top level, i.e., on those who are in a position to take decisions, should also be a part of this strategy. Voluntary organisations, while performing an advocacy role, need to develop effective strategies addressing all the three levels. Only then would they be able to attract the attention of policymakers to neglected issues and/or the bypassed sections.

Secondly, the role that I would emphasise for NGOs is that of the role of 'protestor.' Organising protest becomes a duty when there is injustice and discrimination, say, violation of human rights and civil liberties. It is not an easy function to perform. Although we claim to have a culture of tolerance, in fact, we as people are intolerant when faced with dissent. It is difficult for us to take protest in the right spirit. More often than not, protest evokes revenge. One has to be prepared for such a situation. To be reconciled to injustice, merely because it could lead to confrontation, would be to weaken the roots of democracy. The dependence of most NGOs on government grants creates another hurdle to organising protest. Even when an organisation does not receive any government help, it would like to keep its doors open and therefore avoids confrontation. The organisations with a mass base can take on the opposition of powerful entities, including the government.

Protest against injustice should not be confined to government actions or its style of functioning. Protest against the sections of the society or individuals who indulge in wrong-doing also becomes necessary. Many a time, protest against vested interests in society is more difficult than that against the government. But the civil society institutions have to be prepared for that.

In my view, organisations of the civil society should not abandon decorum and dignity while organising protest. By taking an extreme adversarial position and considering our opponent an enemy, we lose our strength. In a society like ours, such restraint is a sign of strength rather than weakness. I grant that a dignified protest could in truth be merely a symbolic one, even amounting to 'shadow boxing'. But, I believe that concerned parties would differentiate between a genuine protest and a pseudo-protest. We have several examples that show that in many situations, protest carried out in a civil manner has proved more effective. Gandhi's experiments in organising protests during our freedom struggle are examples which prove my point.

Advocacy and protest are essential—the former in creating consensus in a democracy and the latter in bringing the marginalised people and issues into the mainstream. The role of 'initiative' is equally important in giving a new dimension to development activities. The approach, 'more of the same' has not proved effective in breaking economic stagnation and enabling the deprived sections to participate in development and partake of its fruits. Both the state and the market are handicapped in evolving new concepts of development or generating new policies and programmes. The state has a limitation because its main executive body—the bureaucracy—is not able to break away from its rule-bound tradition. The market agents are motivated by profit and therefore cannot take initiatives whose results are of a long-term nature and have an element of uncertainty. The social and voluntary organisations connected with the people can play the role of innovators more efficiently. These organisations can tap the energy of the common people, activate the passive resources and take risks, keeping in view the long-term objectives. The initiative undertaken by these organisations acquires greater importance when the innovation is aimed at affecting the mainstream action and thinking. If the latter objective is to be served, NGO should develop a strategy to cooperate with the state and market institutions.

It needs to be emphasised that the organisations that choose the path of advocacy, protest and initiative for themselves are expected to be committed to the basic concepts of democracy, namely transparency and accountability, and internal democracy. nstitutions that themselves are run undemocratically cannot strengthen it.

11

Academics as Activists

An Indian Perspective on Action Research in Rural Development[*]

In developing societies, there are demands on academics that go far beyond their role in the classroom and laboratory. An academician may have to act as an advisor to the ruling powers, a spokesman for dissenting groups, a catalytic agent for mobilising people for group action, an activist in the struggle of the oppressed and the like. The call to perform these various roles may come from organised agencies or informal groups. Or the circumstances may so develop that he is inspired, or forced, to respond. In recent years, in a number of developing countries, academics have started taking keen interest in the activities centred around groups of the rural and the urban poor. The extent of involvement varies from close observation and in-depth studies, to active participation in the struggle of the downtrodden masses for better life. Somewhere in that range is a position where the academician, while involved in activities of the chosen group, consciously uses such involvement as an opportunity to learn the nature and dynamics of societal behaviour with a view to convey the knowledge to his peers, his students or to the public at large. Involvement of this nature usually goes in the name of 'action research'.

The concept, however, needs to be elaborated and its implications underlined. I will attempt this in the first section of this paper. In the second section, I will briefly outline the nature of involvement of academics in rural development activities in India. In the third and the last section, comparative advantages and disadvantages of academics in the action-research situations will be highlighted. It may be clarified

* This paper is largely based on the author's Bhaikaka Memorial Lecture delivered in Vallabh Vidhyanagar, August 1979.

at the outset that the following discussion is centred around the role of academics who are affiliated to training and research institutions and continue to perform their institutional obligations as teachers and researchers.

I

Action Research: Distinctive Features

Social scientists dealing with contemporary problems of development have recognised the need for meaningfully integrating the observed data with the background knowledge, particularly in situations "in which statistical information matters less than the knowledge of regularities in the behaviour of people or in the character of institutions" (Helmer and Rescher, 1959). For a long time, they have been experimenting with the iterative process of learning and implementing in varied organisational settings. This has been attempted through simulation, games, role playing, etc., and also, in a few cases, through interventions in the live situations. One of the earliest, and better known, experiments in action research in India was conducted by a group of management experts under the leadership of A.K. Rice in a textile mill in Ahmedabad. The objective was to create a conducive atmosphere for raising labour productivity (Rice, 1958). In a recent article, Dey (1978) has cited a few similar experiments in the organised industries as well as in the small communities.

Most of the action-research attempts by the management experts are in the area of organisation development (OD) in medium-to-large business enterprises. In these situations, the tasks are better defined and the knowledge base is more dependable. The design of the OD interventions are, relatively speaking, straightforward. This is not so when it comes to the interventions at the communal level, as our understanding of communities, especially the poorer ones, is rather superficial. Yet it is only through active involvement, i.e., through participation in group action that such an understanding will mature. An iterative process of learning and implementing is the distinct feature of action research. Pareek (1978) has described this process succinctly: "Based on the limited understanding of the subject matter, interventions are designed to affect a change. The data generated from this effort at change further enhances understanding about the subject matter." Equal emphasis on experience and reflections, on conceptualisation and implementation, is the essential ingredient of action research (Tandon, 1979).

Action research has distinct epistemological and methodological bases, but it goes much beyond these distinctions. It has an ideological underpinning. This will be clear if we examine the nature of action research in the context of rural development in the Third World countries. During the last few years, rural development has acquired a specific connotation in these countries, which is shared by a large number of individuals and agencies—ranging from multilateral aid agencies to activists involved in the group actions. According to this concept, the objective of rural development is to bring the bypassed and marginalised sections of rural poor into the mainstream of social and economic progress in such a way that the efforts are sustainable (Vyas, 1977).

Thus viewed, rural development has the rural poor as the main focus and principal beneficiaries. In a situation of acute scarcity of resources, development of the poor would mean, among other things, the poor claiming a bigger share in the productive resources. Even when new resources are created, the interest of the poor will have to be safeguarded lest these increments too are pre-empted by well-off and well-entrenched sections. There is clearly a conflict of interest among those who would get their share, or even more, in the ordinary course of development, and those who will have to struggle to get their legitimate part. The approach to conflict resolution may differ—from 'change of heart' to 'elimination of antagonists'—but the fact of conflict cannot be assumed away. The academics who wish to be involved in action research in rural development will have to take a partisan attitude.

On this, there is a fair degree of unanimity. There is another aspect of action research that might not have been consciously grasped by the academicians. So long as an academic is not forsaking his principal function of a teacher and a researcher, his involvement has an implication for the strategy of change. Bringing the understanding of aspirations, handicaps and struggles of the poor into a classroom, or a classroom-like situation, presumes (a) one is interested in creating a wider awareness and a social consensus; and (b) one believes that such consensus will be instrumental in redesigning developmental strategies. There is thus an implicit faith in creating, what might be called, a lateral pressure, as distinct from pressure from below and above. This aspect of action research is as much value loaded as the fact of academics lending support to poor-oriented development strategy. If one is not interested in 'educating'—granted that the act of educating will involve, first, an act of learning—one has no role to play qua academics.

These value premises impart certain distinctive features to the action research methodology, as well as a distinct orientation to the action researchers. Briefly these are:

- *Long-term Commitment*: Learning through the action research method is likely to be time consuming. A researcher has to act as a participant observer. For any outsider to observe the group dynamics and influence the action of the group would require constant involvement with group activities for a long time. Action research cannot be conducted through proxies or by 'development tourists'.
- *Utility to Action Group*: Since the research is based on action, one naturally identifies and delineates the action group one would like to be associated with. But from the group's point of view, the researcher has to establish his usefulness in furthering the group's interest. No one likes to be treated merely as an object of enquiry without some prospects of tangible benefits. It is not surprising that academics having useful skills, e.g., medical practitioners or engineers, find an easy entry in the action groups. In order to be acceptable, a researcher will have to be clear about the contribution he can make. This implies prior reflection on the nature of group action and the comparative strength one has in facilitating group's tasks.
- *Extent of Intervention*: The intervention by an action researcher would understandably vary in form and content.

It is clear though that if one is interested in learning through participation, one would not dominate the action. The academician's role would be to suggest the line of action, persuade people to act on those lines, and take his share of responsibilities. His role is neither of a leader nor that of a mere consultant.

- *Responsibility for Intervention*: There is a sharp distinction between an action researcher and a manipulator. The former is conscious of the fact that he is dealing with human beings who will face certain consequences while acting on his advice. He would, therefore, take responsibility for his action. In other words, action research presumes a personal stake in the action on the part of the researcher.
- *Responsibility as a Researcher*: The researcher will have to constantly remind himself that his major role continues to be that of a researcher. In that role, one is expected to retain certain objectivity to assess validity and efficacy of the interventions. Admittedly, there is a thin line dividing the action researcher and the full-fledged activist, but such distinction is meaningful only if action research is pursued as a method of learning and enquiry.

II

Indian Academics and Action Research

Various roles that the academics have assumed in the developing societies were also performed by a sizeable number of Indian scholars in the pre-Independence days. They were in the mainstream of the freedom movement and heeded the call of the leadership to perform a variety of tasks. However, it was the genius of Gandhi who could prescribe for the academics a role which is quite close to that of an action researcher. One of the important instruments used by Gandhi during the freedom struggle was the boycott of state-run and state-supported educational institutions. The alternative he offered was the nationalist schools run on the principle of basic education, i.e., a craft-centred education with an ethical bias. The teachers and the students who responded to his call volunteered to teach in these schools—most of which were primary (*buniyadi*) or upper primary (*uttar buniyadi*) schools. Soon institutions of higher learning patterned on the same lines were established. Two of the most famous ones were the Gujarat Vidyapeeth and the Kashi Vidyapeeth; there were several other spread all over the country. The basic schools and the nationalist institutions of higher learning flourished more in the western part of India where Gandhi's influence was particularly strong.

Most of the nationalist schools were in the rural areas. These were residential schools and were known as *ashram shalas*. They made special efforts to educate downtrodden sections of the rural population, the *harijans* and the tribals. The teachers who were running these institutions could not remain immune from problems of the society in the midst of which they were located and functioning. The curricula developed for these schools were evolved from relevant experiences and observations of the educators. Although these institutions emphasised the Gandhian drill to the limits of orthodoxy, they also made both the instructors and the scholars keenly aware of the Indian reality. Quite a few among the educationists, men like J.C. Kumarppa and J.B. Kripalani, rose to national eminence. These institutions provided not only the cadre but the elite of the national struggle, especially in the non-metropolitan areas.

An important role performed by the educators in these institutions was that of mobilisation of rural masses in various active phases of the freedom movement. It was quite natural that they could not forsake the responsibility of assisting poorer sections in availing their legitimate rights. For example, when the first popular ministry in erstwhile Bombay State enacted a tenancy reform legislation, some of the nationalist institutions in Gujarat and Maharashtra actively supported the tenants and sharecroppers in securing rights of permanent occupancy and provisions for reduced rent provided under the legislation. Thus, the hallmark of the nationalist education was to learn from the people, partake in their struggles (adhering, of course, to Gandhian methods) and to kindle awakening among the rural masses.

These institutions, unfortunately, spent their elan soon after the Independence. The policies pursued by the governments of India after Independence made formal education much more attractive than the nationalist education. The grants and subsidies to the latter continued but it was clear these institutions were living on borrowed time. By the early 1950s, the spirit of national education had died down, though a few institutions have continued to struggle valiantly, adapt themselves to the newer challenges, and change over to neo-Gandhian values. Such attempts are few and far between. With the virtual death of the nationalist education movement, collapsed the first, and massive, effort to ascribe the role of 'trinity' to the educator: learner, instructor and implementor. But it must be admitted that in its heyday, the nationalist education system had features quite close to the attributes of action research. People who were part of this educational stream had long-term commitment, clear ideological orientation, a sense of responsibility and an attitude of learner instructor.

The recent revival of the interest of academics in action research as a pedagogical device—with its attendant ideological and epistemological correlates—owes its origin to three distinct sources, each prompting an intense involvement of the academics not only in the understanding of the realities of rural life, but also in the struggle of the people against injustice. In a recent survey Roy (1982) has described various phases of such involvement from a radical, or what he calls counter-ideology, perspective. The first and the most intense type of involvement is that of the academics who have joined radical activist movements, such as Naxalbari, or later on Bhumi Sena and Chhatra Yuva Sangharsh Vahini. For obvious reasons, academics involved in these movements have no desire to come back to classrooms. They have fully identified themselves with their chosen movements and organisations.

The second group of academics are involved in a mass awakening and conscientisation process. The most organised and effective are the scientific workers who find that 'science and technology have become the hand maidens of a few privileged persons." They would not rest content with 'demystifying' the science, but would like to use it as an instrument of class struggle in favour of the poor. People's Science

Movement in Kerala is the most notable among these groups. There are active groups of scientific workers in Maharashtra, Gujarat, West Bengal, Delhi and elsewhere. Other professional groups (those of lawyers, medical practitioners and engineers being more prominent among them) have come into existence in various part of the country with the objective of understanding the relationship between their discipline and societal action, with a distinct ideological commitment and involvement in the poor-oriented programmes.

In the third category, and one which comes closest to our idea of action researchers, is the academic who perceives his role basically as an instructor or a researcher, but realises that a well-informed involvement with activities of the poor will enhance his understanding and will make him more effective in performing his chosen tasks. Generally these individuals are affiliated to formal educational institutions. We can identify three principal models of such involvement.

- The academics who are interested in rural development, particularly in observing and contributing to action, form separate institutions, which are solely devoted to action research in rural or urban development.
- A group of faculty, or an individual faculty, takes leave of absence for a year or two and works with an action group. The academics bring to bear their own expertise in the service of the rural community, and imbibe the realities of the rural situation by close observation and involvement.
- In existing institutions, particularly among the larger ones, academics desirous of taking part in action research are granted some relief from routine tasks, are insulated from the normal institutional chores and discipline and are provided with infrastructural support to work in the rural areas. They remain part of the parent institution, continue to perform in some measure their academic task, but mainly act as liaison between the action groups and the academic community.

The next section is devoted to the role that this group of academics can perform, the handicaps they suffer from and the advantages they enjoy. This section draws on the author's experience as a participant in a rural development action research project in a backward tribal region in South Gujarat. The project came to be known as the Dharampur Project.[1]

III

Academics as Activists

While discussing the role of academics as action researchers, the underlying attributes of action research must be clearly understood. If there is a clear understanding of the role and the tasks of researchers in this setting, the academics can enjoy several comparative advantages. We discovered this, and also the specific handicaps of the academician as a participant in group action, in the Dharampur Project.

To start with, it is much easier for the academics to gain an entry and acceptability in any community. Notwithstanding prevailing cynicism, academics affiliated to the institutions of higher learning are considered *ipso facto*, 'respectable' individuals. In fact, so-called backward societies attach even greater value to learning. The scholars and academics enjoy a very favourable, rather privileged, position in these societies. The same is true, although for other reasons, of the relationship between the academics and the bureaucrats, and particularly that between the academicians and the bureaucrats working in non-metropolitan centres. For an official working in remote areas, e.g., a Collector of a district or a District Development Officer, the college and university teachers are among those few individuals with whom he can interact with relative case. In the *moffusil* places where they are posted, academics who are equally well- or better-educated individuals constitute that part of the milieu to which they, the bureaucrats, can easily relate (provided they do not feel threatened by the easy accessibility which the academics may enjoy with their superiors). Generally, people as well as the bureaucrats treat academics with a degree of respect, which they may not accord to other professionals.

---

1. For the objective, strategy and methodology, see Vyas *et al.* (1976).

The academics can, generally, maintain an objectivity and independence which several other, including the functionaries of large voluntary organisations, find difficult to retain. Although ideological biases of the academics are always present, the level of abstraction at the ideal plane and the large gap between ideological premises and realities at the field level make it possible to keep such predilections in the background and permit them to take a more pragmatic view.

The objectivity enjoyed by the academics is coupled with the freshness of approach in resolving problems. In this respect, they provide a contrast to the bureaucrats who find it difficult to depart from set approaches and procedures. The 'freshness' of the academics can be related to two sources; firstly, unlike bureaucrats, they are not 'prisoners of precedents.' In dealing with issues and problems, they can afford to experiment and innovate. Secondly, their contact with the world of ideas refines their ability to conceptualise; it exposes them to new understanding, and prompts them to propose innovative approaches. These approaches may be dubbed academic, but they reflect accumulated experience and insights.

The academics have clear advantages in establishing links with other organisationsm particularly research and developmental bodies. An atmosphere of mutual trust can be created and the spirit of camaraderie evoked. This is particularly true when the work of various academic institutions is complementary rather than competitive. In the Dharampur Project, at every stage, we sought and received very good support from different institutions. The local college as well as the Bureau of Economics and Statistics of the state government assisted us in conducting large-scale census and also sample surveys of the households. The Gujarat Agricultural University's Navasari campus could be involved in the detailed soil mapping and other technical work pertaining to land-use planning. The sociological and anthropological background of various tribes residing in the area could be studied with the help of various specialised institutions. For selecting a portfolio of labour-intensive forestry development programmes, we could receive very good support from the Forestry Research Institute. I venture to suggest that for the developmental activities, cooperation from other institutions would be more readily forthcoming should the request come from an academic institution rather than from the bureaucratic establishments.

The point most in favour of the academics' involvement in rural development activities is their easy rapport with the younger people. They deal with young people and understand them. The academic institutions will find it easier to mobilise 'student power' for initiating developmental activities. On many occasions, the academics may also enlist the help of past students now occupying key positions in services, trade, commerce, industry, etc., in the selected area. Such contacts are invaluable for obtaining results.

To sum up, acceptability by bureaucrats and the public at large, objective outlook and innovative approach, possibility of building bridges between different institutions, and capability of mobilising young and enthusiastic support constitute favourable features of an action programme that involves the academics.

At the same time, the academics have serious handicaps in participating in an action-research programme for the rural poor in developing societies like ours. These handicaps are over and above the overriding constraint imposed by social background of the teachers and researchers, which is generally different from the group of people they are going to work with. It is important to underline these limitations because in our enthusiasm to involve academics from educational institutions, particularly from the institutions of higher learning, in rural development, we are likely to forget these.

The major limitation arises due to the conflict between career goals of the researcher and his ideological predilections. The career advancement of academics is linked with the research of the conventional type, publications in academic journals, performance in the classroom, participation in seminars, symposia and contribution through committees and commissions. Most of these are facilitated by single-minded devotion to the chosen field of specialisation. The involvement in action research does not directly subserve the career goals. More often than not, ideological commitment of the faculty serves as the mainspring for involvement in rural development activities. Such commitments do not last long once the constraints to career advance become obvious. It is not surprising, therefore, to find that most academics actively involved in rural development are either too young, and presumably not overly concerned with their career prospects, or those elderly scholars who have already established their academic reputation.

By the nature of their training, and also because of the traditions in certain disciplines, particularly in social sciences, an academic is a lone wolf. (This may not apply to the teaching and research work in natural sciences where in several areas teamwork has become a necessity.) There are few instances of sustained and lasting team work by the academics even in narrow academic pursuits. Activities included in the rural development programmes require sustained teamwork. Without a formal binding mechanism, the academics do not find it easy to work as a team.

A similar handicap becomes obvious while dealing with a multitude of agencies and actors. By training, a scholar likes to relate himself to a known, identified, client or client groups. When demands are emanating from diverse sections with a variety of constraining and facilitating factors, his single-end, purist approach does not help in forging a strategy composed of different strands. In this respect, bureaucrats or politicians have a distinct advantage, as by training and aptitude, they can simultaneously deal with different groups in varied circumstances.

A similar difficulty is faced by the academies in taking decisions that have political connotations. Again, his training and background do not equip him to cope with the situation of open conflict, of power sharing, of settlements by bargaining and trade-offs. Whenever a situation of multiple goals and contending factions emerge, he is clearly at a disadvantage. And these situations are at the core of rural reality.

In spite of the handicaps noted above, the current mood of academics to champion the cause of the rural poor by active involvement with poor-oriented programmes is a welcome one. It will help the rural development programmes for the reasons I have referred to earlier. It will also help academics to grasp the rural realities and bringing that knowledge to the classroom.

There are two major expectations when academics enter this arena. It is expected in the first place that their involvement is not sporadic nor purely research-oriented. Their commitments should be lasting and their involvement should be clearly to facilitate action in favour of the rural poor. The academics' role may not be the same as that of full-fledged activists, but in the action research context, his role is essentially that of facilitating action in desired directions. Consequently, he cannot abdicate his responsibility to the group. At the same time, so long as he operates from the base of a university, a college or a research institution, it is expected that the experience gained while facilitating the change will be incorporated in the teaching and research material. If either of these two conditions are not fulfilled, there is no particular advantage in involving academics in an action research programme for rural development.

References

Dey, Nitish (1978). "Action Research as a Learing Strategy", Paper submitted to the *ICSSR Seminar on Action Research*, Lonavala, October (*Memo*).

Helmer, O. and N. Rescher (1959). "On the Epistomology of the Inexact Sciences", *Management Science*. October.

Pareek, Udai (1978). "Action Research in Organisations", Paper presented at the *Second IIMA Seminar on Management Research*, Ahmedabad, January (*Memo*).

Rice, A.K. (1958). *Productivity and Social Organization: The Ahmedabad Experiment*. London: Tavistock Publication.

Roy, Dunu (1983). "Between Dogma and Debate", *BUILD Background Papers* Series, No. 5.

Tandon, Rajesh (1978). "Action Research: Assumptions and Practice", Paper submitted to the *ICSSR Seminar on Action Research*, Lonavala. October (*Memo*).

Vyas, V.S, T.K. Maulik, B.M. Desai and Raujit Gupta (1976). *Rural Development for Rural Poor—Dharampur Project, Part I: The Setting*. Ahmedabad: Center for Management in Agriculture, IIMA.

———. (1977). "Rural Develpment: Some Issues and Approaches", *IIMA Working Paper* No. 163. Ahmedabad: IIMA. June.